Writer's
GUIDE TO
Internet
Resources

Writer's

GUIDE TO

Internet

Resources

Vicky Phillips
Cindy Yager

MACMILLAN·USA

Macmillan General Reference
A Simon & Schuster Macmillan Company
1633 Broadway
New York, NY 10019-6785

Macmillan Publishing books may be purchased for business or sales promotional use.
For information please write: Special Markets Department, Macmillan Publishing
USA, 1633 Broadway, New York, NY 10019.

An Arco Book

MACMILLAN is a registered trademark of Macmillan, Inc.

ARCO is a registered trademark of Simon & Schuster, Inc.

Library of Congress Number: 97-070667
International Standard Book Number: 0-02-861882-3

Manufactured in the United States of America

10 9 8 7 6 5 4 3 2 1

Dedication

This book is for my grandmother, Anabelle England, of Brownstown, Indiana, who read to me incessantly when I was a child—which is how I got the rather peculiar idea that life exists to be written about in the first place. This book is also for my mother, June Phillips, of Bedford, Indiana. (Thank you, Momma, for having the courage of heart to let me make my own way—mistakes and all—in this sometimes woe-begotten world.)

Vicky Phillips

This effort is dedicated to two people who are as responsible as I am for my success: my parents. Though I only had him for a few short years, my father, Paul, instilled in me a deep love and respect for education and reading. Thank you, Daddy. Whatever else may have transpired, my mother, Sheila, always believed in me just a little bit more than I could. Thank you, Mom.

Cindy Yager

Table of Contents

Introduction

"Trying to find something on the Internet is like trying to find the bathroom in a house with 10,000 doors—all of them unmarked."

—Anonymous Posting to an Internet Mailing List

The Internet. Free, instant, inexhaustible information. Great stuff for cash-strapped writers of all persuasion. Government databases, world-class libraries, accessible experts, publisher's catalogs, electronic book super stores, news desktop delivery services, writers' workshops, electronic book reading clubs, and lucrative freelance writing opportunities. For writers, the Internet is a Royal Road to Informational Oz.

Well, not quite.

The Net promises instant opportunity for writers. This is a valid promise, but only if you know how to get online and where to head once this vital electronic connection has been made. Plug in your modem and dial up the Net. A couple of mouse clicks later, you're online posting your stories to a freelancer's clearinghouse for editors to peruse and purchase. Then you're off to scour Usenet newsgroups, the bulletin boards of cyberspace, to locate an expert or two to interview for that piece you're doing on elder abuse. Last stop: publishers' online catalogs to investigate which houses are publishing new titles this spring in your specialty areas.

So, what's the problem? The problem is that before you can use the Internet you have to know what it is and where the informational gold is hidden. There are millions of places to go online. And we do mean millions. You can't just get on the Information Superhighway and start driving. Well, you can, and some hearty souls do, but traveling the vastness of cyberspace without a map and a compass is somewhat like deciding to run the Iditarod dog sled race in a swim suit with a team of toy poodles to pull you along. It could be done, but we'd advise against it if you really want to get somewhere interesting in the long run.

We started drawing our own map of where to go and what to do online back in 1990—during the Dark Ages of the Net. A time when we fearlessly rode the primordial Net on amazing technological dinosaurs—tiny, toylike computers that had virtually no power or reach when compared to today's amazing machines. As we rode, we drew freehand maps to writing hot spots and the best ways to use the Net as freelance writers. Our notes and maps have come together in the shape of this guide to the Internet for writers of all types.

In writing this book, we've tried to make it as reader friendly as possible. Hence, you won't find a lot of techno-argot in this guide. Whenever possible, we have used simple metaphor rather than techno-argot to explain how or why some Net tool or procedure works. We assume that when you came looking for this book you came looking for a companion guide that would lay out the treasures of the Net as clearly as possible. This is what we have tried to give you. We hope we succeeded.

In writing this guide we felt that, rather than just giving you a directory of places to visit online, we should also highlight crucial industry trends for you. The Net is changing the very nature of media and publishing as we write. Issues like royalties on electronic rights, electronic book marketing, and writing for the new media markets are issues that did not even exist a few years ago. Now these issues are at the heart of the everyday world of writers and publishers— essential, in fact, to their very economic existence. Each chapter sketches out industry trends so that you can stay aware of what's changing in the world of publishing as it goes increasingly electronic.

Another vital feature of our guide is that we tell you up front where to go to find more of the same sort of thing that we have written about. For example, we don't attempt to list all of the 2,000 newspapers worldwide that now have online editions. Instead, we highlight the most interesting online editions, pointing out how online editions differ from their newsstand siblings. We then list the best master newspaper indexes or directories that exist online. This way, you can actually learn how to find newspapers online long after what we have told you about specific papers has faded from your mind.

We give you this kind of "how-to" data because we think it's true that if you give a man a fish you may quiet his hunger for a day, but if you teach him to fish you've taught him to feed himself for a lifetime. We want you to be able to fish the Net for yourself, so to speak. Our guide is written to help you painlessly along.

The Internet is a networked collection of millions of computers. It is the product of the efforts of millions of people. As such the Internet is always under construction. New sites are being constructed and put online daily. Likewise, many sites are being taken down, altered, or added to every day. This state of constant change is what makes the Internet both intriguing and frustrating.

It is likely that some of the sites listed in this book will have disappeared or been altered by the time you get around to visiting them online. It is also likely that some services, like the fee-based news search services outlined in Chapter 5, "Researching Online: Reference Works and News Search Services," may have changed their rates by the time this book reaches you. All the information in this book was current when the book went to print, nonetheless, you should be prepared for the fact that the Internet is prone to rapid change.

Change is not a bad thing, but flux can be frustrating when you need to find something—and quickly! If you can't find something listed in this book, visit one of the many search engines that are available free online. These search engines will allow you to search for any lost or missing sites. If you are not familiar with how to search for things online, Internet search engines and how they work are outlined in Chapter 14, "Finding Your Way Through Cyberspace: Power-Using Internet Search Engines and Indexes."

If you are not very familiar with the online world, you may want to start by reading Part III, "A Writer's Primer to Using the Internet." The primer explains the basic terminology and tools for online travel. If you have already mastered the basics of getting online, you can start with Part I, "What's Out There for Writers." Each chapter in Part I covers a different online area of interest, from how to subscribe and participate in electronic writers' workshops to how to secure freelance online writing assignments.

If you are somewhat familiar with the Internet and are looking to hook up your home or office computer to a permanent Internet access provider, you can learn about this process and how to select the best Internet service provider (ISP) by reading Part II, "The Commercial Online Services." Popular online services like America Online and CompuServe are described in this part of the book. If you already subscribe to one of these services, Part II gives you a helpful look at the places that writers commonly frequent within each of these services.

That's about it. We hope this guide serves you as planned—as a Yellow Brick Road that leads to the heart of your very own Informational Oz.

If you have any questions or comments, feel free to e-mail us or to drop by our resource centers on the World Wide Web, Writers@Work (SM) **http:// www.together.net/~lifelong/writers.html** or the Adult Education & Distance Learner's Resource Center **http://www.together.net/~lifelong**.

Writers@Work
Vicky Phillips and Cindy Yager,
Lifelong Learning
E-mail: **LifeLearn@aol.com**

PART I

What's Out There for Writers

CHAPTER 1

Getting Your Message Out: *E-Mail, Mailing Lists, and Electronic Newsletters*

Once you've mastered e-mail, the simplest tool of the Internet, you can achieve some amazing things as a writer. This chapter outlines what e-mail is and how it can be used to access a host of online writing opportunities.

You can use e-mail to send inexpensive queries to magazine publishers who reside around the world. Or you can use it to send an overnight note to your agent. It can even be harnessed to allow you to talk with other writers or journalists via special Internet mailing lists.

E-mail can also be used to participate in grassroots writing workshops. You can polish your craft via e-mail without ever leaving the comfort of your keyboard. You can send your screenplay or novel for critiquing, around the globe, in seconds, via e-mail. Finally, plain old e-mail can be used to receive informative, free electronic newsletters like "Inklings," a bimonthly newsletter for writers on the Internet.

E-Mail: What It Is and How to Use It

E-mail, or electronic mail, allows you to create messages on your personal computer, then send these messages over phone wires to another computer. In order to send and receive e-mail you need three things. First, you need a computer equipped with software designed to let you compose e-mail. This is usually called *communications software*. You can compose e-mail in any number of special e-mail programs, like Eudora, or in the software provided by commercial online services like America Online and CompuServe. We use Eudora to compose and send our e-mail because it is easy to use and versions of it are offered free by Internet service providers themselves (see below). We also like the fact that Eudora is named after the writer Eudora Welty in honor of her famous short story, "How I Found Myself at the P.O." or post office.

Next, you need a connection that will allow you to send electronic messages over the phone lines across the Internet. This is called an Internet service provider, or ISP. This connection can be made for you by a commercial service like America Online, or you can sign up with a local or national dial-up service like Netcom.

Finally, you need a modem, a device that literally translates your typed words into electronic—re: modulated, for modem—impulses and sends them off over the phone wires to a remote receiving computer.

How to Read an E-Mail Address

When you send a letter by surface mail—or *snail mail* as it is termed in the online world—you must address it correctly. The same is true of e-mail. To send an e-mail you must know the e-mail address of the recipient.

Surface mail addresses contain several lines of delivery information: the person's name, street address, state, and country. Similarly, e-mail addresses contain several levels of delivery information. These levels allow computer networks to deliver your mail correctly. E-mail addresses are easy to understand if you think of them as regular addresses and read them accordingly. Study this e-mail address for a moment: cyager@smcvt.edu.

Can you make any sense of it?

The first part of any e-mail address is often the person's name or an acronym for the group or department you are trying to reach. "Cyager," here, stands for Cindy Yager, one of the authors of this book. In our example, we are sending e-mail to Cindy Yager.

The "@" symbol is a crucial part of any e-mail address. It literally says, send this e-mail to the person or department located "at" the organization or server name that follows. In our example, we are sending e-mail to Cindy Yager "at" "smcvt," computer shorthand for Saint Michael's College (smc) in Vermont (vt).

The last part of an e-mail address is called the *domain*. The domain code reveals the type of organization you are writing to. Common domain codes are as follows.

com = commercial

edu = educational

mil = military

net = network

org = nonprofit organization

gov = government

In our example, we are sending e-mail to Cindy Yager at St. Michael's College, which is an "edu," or educational organization. If she worked for the military, the last part of her e-mail address would have been "mil." The last part of an international e-mail address is sometimes a country code. "UK" is often the last part of an e-mail address in the United Kingdom. E-mail addresses in the United States do not normally end in a country code. Instead, they end in one of the domain codes listed above.

When we give you e-mail addresses or other computer instructions in this book, we sometimes put them inside brackets: <cyager@smcvt.edu>. We do this so you can tell that we mean this to be an e-mail address or a computer instruction. When you type the e-mail address into the "TO" field of an actual e-mail, or when you type a computer command, leave out the brackets.

Internet Mailing Lists

Sending e-mail to one person is fine. But what if you want to use e-mail to chat with a group of people about a particular topic on an ongoing basis? What if you want to join an ongoing discussion about freelance writing with other freelance writers, for example?

You can do this by subscribing to an automated Internet mailing list, often mistakenly referred to by the generic term, listserv. (There are, in fact, three mailing lists for freelance writers, all described in detail later in this chapter.)

To join an electronic mailing list, you subscribe to the list using e-mail. To do this, you send e-mail to the listserv or program that manages the list. A listserv is an automated mailing program, installed on a main computer, often at a college or university. Programs that manage electronic mailing lists go by several names. Listserv, a particular kind of program, is the most common. Majordomo, listproc, mailbase, and mailserv are others.

Programs like listserv automatically receive and redistribute e-mail messages sent to a central computer address. There are more than 70,000 electronic mailing lists or discussion forums in the English language. All you have to do is find an electronic mailing list that is dedicated to a topic that interests you—like screenwriting, computer-assisted reporting, or romance writing—and then subscribe to it using e-mail.

Once you have subscribed to a list, you will begin to receive e-mail messages from the other members of the list as the listserv goes about its task of redistributing, or "exploding," the e-mail sent to it back out to subscribers.

As a subscriber, you can post e-mail to the stream of discussion traffic for others to read and comment on. Every day, when you log on to read your mail, you will receive e-mail from the others who subscribe to the list you have joined. You can join the discussions in progress by e-mailing your thoughts back to the list address.

How Do Writers Use Lists?

Writers can use lists in several crucial money- and time-saving ways. We've used lists for the following purposes:

- **Writing Workshops** Some lists, like The Writing Workshop, operate as virtual workshops. We've submitted short stories to these lists for critique and analysis by other writers. In return, we've received better stories and formed delightful electronic friendships with other writers.

- **Expert Interviews**   Industry experts are often impossible to get on the phone. They are much easier to access via e-mail. When we were writing an article on the ways online magazines differ from their newsstand counterparts, we subscribed to the mailing list Online News. Here, we were able to chat with editors who were designing online magazines.

- **Career Enhancement and Freelancing**   We've received numerous freelance assignments from editors who've read our postings to lists and who were impressed enough with our comments to query us about writing for them. Lists like the Computer Book Publishing List often contain announcements from editors looking for specialists to author chapters for upcoming books.

- **Informational Resources**   When we were thinking of self-syndicating a column to weekly newspapers, we learned from the Computer-Assisted Reporting List that several excellent indexes or directories to weekly newspapers were available online. We visited these indexes and pulled newspaper mailing addresses and editors' names off the Web. We then used this information to send out queries by surface mail.

Subscribing

Subscribing to a list is as easy as sending an e-mail message. Remember, when you subscribe to a list you are almost always sending e-mail to a machine—not a person. For this reason, you need to use commands that can be read by the software program that is managing your particular list.

Instructions for how to subscribe to any particular list are given later in our directory of mailing lists. In general, a listserv-managed list will recognize the written command "subscribe," followed by the name of the list or its computer-readable acronym ("scrnwrit") and your name ("vicky phillips") directly to the e-mail address of the listserv that manages the list.

For example, to subscribe to the Screenwriting Discussion List, a forum for screenwriters, you'd send the e-mail message "subscribe scrnwrit vicky phillips" directly to the listserv that manages that list, <listserv@tamvm1.tamu.edu>.

You will receive an e-mail from the listserv confirming that your subscription efforts were successful. Keep this welcome message because it contains instructions on how to unsubscribe or sign off the list as well as how to do other, more complicated tasks like use e-mail commands to search the archives of the list for previous discussions that might interest you.

Using List Commands

Because mailing lists are automated, you can perform many functions using simple computer commands. The welcome message will spell out e-mail commands you can send to the list for automated assistance. One very helpful command, which listserv programs understand, is the "digest" command. Some lists have only a few subscribers, and others have hundreds of participants. The higher the subscription rate, the more frequent the e-mail traffic you'll receive in your box. If a list puts out 75 e-mail messages a day, you may want to send the list an e-mail command to send each day's e-mail to you strung together in digest form. For example, the Computer-Assisted Reporting & Research List (CARR-L) is a moderate-volume list, redistributing about 25 messages a day. It can be received in digest form by sending the command "set carr-l digest" to the address of the listserv that manages this list, <listserv@ulkyvm.louisville.edu>. These and other commands, like how to search the CARR-L archives online, are detailed in the CARR-L welcome message.

Moderated Lists

Many lists operate unchecked by a human hand. A central computer distributes messages without a care as to content. If a debate breaks out, members of the list jointly try to resolve it. Other lists have moderators. The moderator is often the person who implemented the list. Some moderators screen all incoming messages, keeping inappropriate messages from appearing on the list. A moderator is especially helpful in keeping unwanted commercial messages off your list and in barring obscene pranksters from membership.

If the list you are subscribing to is moderated, this will be explained in the welcome message. The name and e-mail address of the list moderator will be stated along with the rules your moderator has sworn to enforce.

Pay attention to these rules. Many workshop-style lists, for example, do not accept erotica for critiquing. A moderator can unsubscribe wayward participants, so take the moderator's role as List-God seriously.

Mailing Lists and Companion World Wide Web Addresses

Another common kind of Internet address is the Web address. The Web is the part of the Internet that allows people to access information online in a rich multimedia format. The Web, or World Wide Web as it is often called (WWW for short), is the part of the Internet that supports rich texts and graphics. The World Wide Web is the most exciting part of the Internet. It is also the most traveled part of the Internet these days.

To access a Web site online, you need to know the Web address. Web addresses are everywhere these days. Like an e-mail address, a Web address makes sense if you know how to read it. World Wide Web addresses always begin with the three little letters "www." For example, our main Web site can be accessed online at **http://www.together.net/~lifelong**. Web addresses are commonly prefaced by the acronym **http**, which stands for hypertext transfer protocol. If you've never been online or are not yet familiar with the World Wide Web, refer to Chapter 15, "Browsing the World Wide Web," for an introduction to this exciting multimedia part of the Internet.

In this chapter we mention the Web and Web addresses because some of the electronic mailing lists that we discuss in detail in this chapter have companion Web sites. These Web sites generally house information about the mailing list and archive the rules for list participation. Companion Web sites may also contain other information that might be of interest to list members.

If a mailing list has a companion Web site it is listed in the directory that follows. For example, the Computer Book Publishing List supports a companion Web site that is accessible online at **http://www.studiob.com**. This Web site is the online home of Studio B, the computer book agency that sponsors the electronic Computer Book Publishing List. The Studio B Web page archives old issues of the Computer Book Publishing List, so anyone can access and read the discussions that have transpired on the Computer Book Publishing List during the last few years. The Web page also houses a great deal of other useful information about computer book publishing and the activities of the sponsoring agency, Studio B.

Locating Lists

New lists start up all the time. Existing lists move from one server to another. Search the following central resources to keep up with lists as they come and go, and to locate new lists in your specialty areas.

Publicly Accessible Mailing Lists (PAML)
http://www.NeoSoft.com:80/internet/paml/bysubj.html

The Publicly Accessible Mailing Lists page is a labor of love by Internet citizen or "netizen" Stephanie da Silva. This first-rate resource chronicles more than 1,500 publicly accessible lists by topic, from abuse to yoga. The great thing about this site is that it catalogs only those lists that are open to the public, so you don't waste time attempting to subscribe to lists that are open only through invitation or private association membership.

Liszt
http://www.liszt.com/

Liszt is a database of more than 70,000 public and private lists.

Tile.Net
http://www.tile.net/

Tile.Net is our favorite master database. The last time we searched for "writing" lists, more than 120 lists popped up. Be forewarned, though, that many of the lists are not open to the public. The majority are private lists. If a list is described as "A writing and research forum for Mr. Chip's Spring '98 Humanities 101a course," it's probably only open to those who appear on Mr. Chip's class roster.

Fought's Finds
http://web.syr.edu/~bcfought/

Professor Barbara Croll Fought, of Syracuse University's Newhouse School of Communication, maintains this one-stop resource directory to Net mailing lists and newsletters in all areas of communication: advertising, communication law, film, journalism, interactive communications, photojournalism, public relations, radio, telecommunications, and broadcasting.

Netiquette—Minding Your Manners

Thirty million people travel on the Internet. Millions more are coming. Like any social group, the Net has evolved a set of do's and don'ts to keep peace among the masses. As in real life, the rules of good etiquette are few and simple. Violation of them can earn you blistering e-mail—called "flames"—or get you exiled from selected Internet communities. Pay heed. Learn to mind your manners.

Rule #1: Do Not Type in Capital Letters   When composing any electronic posting, refrain from typing in capitals. Capital letters are read as "shouts" by receivers. And shouting, as we all know, is rude.

Rule #2: Don't Post Anything You Wouldn't Want Momma to Read   Many mailing lists are archived online. If you're having a bad day and post something as off-color as your mood, that posting is not gone when you log off for the day. Not hardly. Several years later, someone could be reading through an online archive only to discover your incredible bad manners.

Rule #3: Don't Be a Flame Thrower   With 30 million cybernauts or cyber-citizens online, you won't be surprised to learn that some percentage of Net cruisers are idiots or bullies—or an unfortunate combination of both. When people start attacking others online it's called *flaming*. It's best to ignore such flames.

Rule #4: Lurk for Awhile   Electronic forums are tribes of a type. Some tribes are very friendly to newcomers—or *newbies* as they are called. Some are not. To discern the tone of any mailing list, try lurking for awhile. Lurking is the term for hanging out and reading a list for a week or two before you actually post anything. When you do post, many consider it proper form that your first post be an introduction of who you are and why you joined the list.

Rule #5: Be Careful about Ads   Advertising on the Net is a hotly debated topic. Most lists ban commercial messages. Some allow commercial messages if they are relevant to the list's topic of discussion. The list's welcome message generally contains a statement on advertising. Under no circumstances should you "spam" lists with commercial announcements. Spamming is the term used to describe what happens when a blatant commercial offer—"Grow Hair in 30 Days!"—is sent unsolicited to all members of a mailing list.

Directory of Writing-Related Mailing Lists

There is a list on every imaginable topic. There are a number of lists that exist solely to discuss the literary works of classic authors. There is an Oscar Wilde list and an Ozian Times list—to discuss Frank Baum's Oz works, of course. There is also a list on antique typewriters and one for fans of movie star Jodie Foster.

With more than 70,000 mailing lists in the English language, we can't chronicle them all. Below are the best and most active writers' lists. The first set of lists includes general discussion forums on topics ranging from book publishing to technical writing. The last section consists of online workshops—places where one can get and give critiques about works in progress.

Books and Book Publishing

Bibliophile
To subscribe, send e-mail to: **biblio-request@smartlink.net**
Type in the body of your e-mail message: **subscribe**
http://www.smartlink.net/~biblio

A highly active list for those who buy, collect, or trade out-of-print books. Subscribers are listed on The Bookshelf, a page on the World Wide Web (WWW) dedicated to rare-book buyers and sellers.

Bookwoman
To subscribe, send e-mail to: **majordomo@vector.casti.com**
Type in the body of your e-mail message: **subscribe bookwoman <your name> <your e-mail address>**

Bookwoman is a reading group dedicated to the discussion of books authored by women.

Computer Book Publishing List
To subscribe, send e-mail to: **list@studiob.com**
Type in the subject line of your e-mail message: **subscribe**
http://www.studiob.com

The Computer Book Publishing List is for publishers, editors, and authors involved in the computer book industry. Back issues and additional information for computer book authors are archived online by the sponsor, Studio B.

EBook-List
To subscribe, send e-mail to: **majordomo@aros.net**
Type in the body of your e-mail message: **subscribe ebook-list**

E-book covers everything about the electronic book publishing industry, including how to develop, produce, and distribute electronic books.

Feminist Bibliography (fem-biblio)
To subscribe, send e-mail to: **listserv@listserv.aol.com**
Type in the body of your e-mail message: **subscribe fem-biblio**

FEM-BIBLIO is an electronic book discussion group for books on the feminine and the spiritual.

Publisher's Marketing Association (pma-l)
To subscribe, send e-mail to: **listserv@shrsys.hslc.org**
Type in the body of your e-mail message: **subscribe <your name>**

The Publisher's Marketing Association hosts this active discussion list dedicated to independent book publishing and marketing in electronic and other forms.

Small-Press
To subscribe, send e-mail to: **majordomo@world.std.com**
Type in the body of your e-mail message: **subscribe small-press**

Small Press is a discussion forum for authors and editors working in the small-press environment, on both books and magazines.

Children's Markets

Children's Writing
To subscribe, send e-mail to: **majordomo@lists.mindspring.com**
Type in the body of your e-mail message: **subscribe childrens-writing**

A discussion list for authors and illustrators of children's works, sponsored by the "Children's Book Insider," an industry newsletter.

Editing

Copyediting-L
To subscribe, send e-mail to: **listproc@cornell.edu**
Type in the body of your e-mail message: **subscribe copyediting-l <your name>**

A high-volume discussion forum for copyeditors and other defenders of the English language.

Freelance Writing

Freelance
To subscribe, send e-mail to: **owner-freelancer@newshare.com**
Type in the body of your e-mail message: **subscribe freelance <your name>**
http://www.newshare.com/

Freelance is a general discussion list for freelance writers. It is sponsored by Newshare, the independent news syndicate that distributes freelance work to Net audiences.

Freelancers
To subscribe, send e-mail to: **two-start@idirect.com**
Type in the body of your e-mail message: **subscribe freelancers**
http://www.twostar.com/lists/

This moderated Canadian forum gives voice to freelance writers and editors wishing to exchange tips and techniques.

National Writers Union—Chat (nwu-chat)
To subscribe, send e-mail to: **majordomo@nwu.org**
Type in the body of your e-mail message: **subscribe nwu-chat**
http://www.nwu.org/nwu/

This is the high-traffic chat and announcement list for members and friends of the National Writers Union (NWU). The NWU is a trade union for freelance writers.

Journalism and Reporting

Computer-Assisted Reporting & Research (CARR-L)
To subscribe, send e-mail to: **listserv@ulkyvm.louisville.edu**
Type in the body of your e-mail message: **subscribe carr-l <your name>**

CARR-L is a top-notch virtual newsroom dedicated to the discussion of how to execute computer-assisted research for writing needs.

Investigative Reporters & Editors (ire-l)
To subscribe, send e-mail to: **listproc@lists.missouri.edu**
Type in the body of your e-mail message: **subscribe ire-l <your name>**
http://www.ire.org/

This is a discussion forum for journalists and editors on legal, ethical, and procedure matters related to investigative reporting. List discussions are archived at the Web site.

Journalism Education (journet-l)
To subscribe, send e-mail to: **listserv@american.edu**
Type in the body of your e-mail message: **subscribe journet-l <your name>**

This is a low-volume general discussion list for journalism instructors and students.

National Institute for Computer-Assisted Reporting (nicar)
To subscribe, send e-mail to: **listproc@lists.missouri.edu**
Type in the body of your e-mail message: **subscribe nicar-l <your name>**
http://www.nicar.org/

A low-volume list from NICAR dedicated to all aspects of computer-assisted and online reporting. Archives are housed at the Web site.

News Research (newslib)
To subscribe, send e-mail to: **listproc@ripken.oit.unc.edu**
Type in the body of your e-mail message: **subscribe newslib <your name>**

A forum for librarians, journalists, and new media workers about online news sources and research tactics.

Online-News
To subscribe, send e-mail to: **majordomo@planetarynews.com**
Type in the body of your e-mail message: **subscribe online-news <your e-mail address>**
http://www.planetarynews.com/online-news.html

A high-volume professional forum for publishers, writers, and developers of electronic editions of newspapers and magazines.

Radio-Television Journalism (rtvj-l)
To subscribe, send e-mail to: **listproc@listserv.umt.edu**
Type in the body of your e-mail message: **subscribe rtvj-l <your name>**

This low-volume list is sponsored by the Radio-Television Division of the Association for Education in Journalism and Mass Communication. The list invites discussion from professionals and students about broadcast journalism.

Society of Professional Journalists (spj-l)
To subscribe, send e-mail to: **listserv@psuvm.psu.edu**
Type in the body of your e-mail message: **subscribe spj-l <your name>**

This list is sponsored by the Society of Professional Journalists (SPJ). Subscribers receive "Press Notes," an electronic newsletter on media industry happenings.

Student Electronic Papers (stuepap)
To subscribe, send e-mail to: **listserv@vm.temple.edu**
Type in the body of your e-mail message: **subscribe stuepap <your name>**

A discussion forum for the nuts-and-bolts issues surrounding the making of an electronic edition of a student paper.

Student Journalism (sj)
To subscribe, send e-mail to: **majordomo@world.std.com**
Type in the body of your e-mail message: **subscribe sj <your e-mail address>**
http://world.std.com/~joeshmoe/sj/

An open discussion forum for teachers and students of journalism. A companion Web site houses archives as well as links to online student journalism projects.

Mystery Markets

DorothyL (Mystery Literature E-Conference)
To subscribe, send e-mail to: **listserv@kentvm.kent.edu**
Type in the body of your e-mail message: **subscribe dorothyl <your name>**

Mystery writers and literature fans subscribe to this active forum to discuss the mystery in short story and novel form.

Gaslight
To subscribe, send e-mail to: **mailserv@mtroyal.ab.ca**
Type in the body of your e-mail message: **subscribe gaslight**
http://www.mtroyal.ab.ca/programs/arts/english/gaslight/welcome.htm

Gaslight is a forum for the discussion of early (1800–1919) crime, mystery, and adventure fiction.

Shortmystery-L
To subscribe, send e-mail to: **majordomo@teleport.com**
Type in the body of your e-mail message: **subscribe shortmystery-l-digest <your e-mail address>**

This list is dedicated to discussions of the mystery in short story or media forms.

Plays, Theater, and Drama

Plays
To subscribe, send e-mail to: **majordomo@world.std.com**
Type in the body of your e-mail message: **subscribe plays**

Plays is dedicated to the discussion of drama and theatrical production concerns. The list serves as an e-mail gateway to the newsgroup rec.arts.theatre.plays.

Stagecraft
To subscribe, send e-mail to: **majordomo@world.std.com**
Type in the body of your e-mail message: **subscribe stagecraft**

This list serves primarily as an e-mail gateway to the newsgroup rec.arts.theatre.stagecraft. Stagecraft is a discussion group for anyone involved in play production, including technical production and atmosphere issues.

Theatre-Misc
To subscribe, send e-mail to: **majordomo@world.std.com**
Type in the body of your e-mail message: **subscribe theatre-misc**

Theatre-misc is the mailing list gateway for the newsgroup of the same name. Subscribers who have e-mail, but lack newsgroup reader capability, may participate in the newsgroup through this mailing list. See Chapter 10, "Searching for Advice and Cameraderie: Usenet Newsgroups," for more information on newsgroups.

Romance Markets

It's Romance
To subscribe, send e-mail to: **majordomo@listserv@prodigy.com**
Type in the body of your e-mail message: **subscribe romance <your e-mail address>**
http://www.goodstuff.prodigy.com/Lists

This active list of romance authors and readers is sponsored by Prodigy, the online service.

Romance Readers Anonymous (RRA-L)
To subscribe, send e-mail to: **listserv@kentvm.kent.edu**
Type in the body of your e-mail message: **subscribe rra-l <your name>**

RRA-L is an active discussion forum for romance aficionados.

Romance Writers (RW-L)
To subscribe, send e-mail to: **listserv@maelstrom.stjohns.edu**
Type in the body of your e-mail message: **subscribe rw-l <your name>**

Romance Writers discuss everything from dealing with editorial rejection to writing romance for senior citizens.

Science Fiction, Fantasy, and Speculative Fiction

Fantasy-L
To subscribe, send e-mail to: **listserv@listserv.aol.com**
Type in the body of your e-mail message: **subscribe fantasy-l <your name>**

This is a low-traffic list for professionals involved in fantasy writing, publishing, or editing.

Literary Science Fiction & Fantasy
To subscribe, send e-mail to: **listproc@loc.gov**
Type in the body of your e-mail message: **subscribe sf-lit <your name>**

A discussion forum on the literary merits and movements within the sci-fi and fantasy genre.

Sci-Fi-Fantasy
To subscribe, send e-mail to: **majordomo@listserv@prodigy.com**
Type in the body of your e-mail message: **subscribe sci-fi-fantasy <your e-mail address>**

A general discussion list on the genre from Prodigy.

Science Fiction & Fantasy Writers (Sfnf-Writers)
To subscribe, send e-mail to: **majordomo@seidel.ncsa.uiuc.edu**
Type in the body of your e-mail message: **subscribe Sfnf <your name>**

This is a high-volume list for writers of science fiction or fantasy. Discussions concerning the business and process of writing are welcome. Works in progress should not be sent to this list but to the companion list, sfnf-critique, listed below in the workshops section.

Science Fiction-Lovers (sf-lovers)
To subscribe, send e-mail to: **sf-lovers-request@rutgers.edu**
Type in the body of your e-mail message: **subscribe sf-lovers**
http://sflovers.rutgers.edu/

A high-volume discussion forum for lovers of science fiction and fantasy media.

United Kingdom Science Fiction Books (uk-sf-books)
To subscribe, send e-mail to: **listproc@lists.pipex.com**
Type in the body of your e-mail message: **subscribe uk-sf-books <your name>**

This list gives voice to readers and writers of quality science fiction, particularly classic and new works from the United Kingdom.

Screenwriting

Film & TV Studies Discussion List (screen-l)
To subscribe, send e-mail to: **listserv@ua1vm.ua.edu**
Type in the body of your e-mail message: **subscribe screen-l <your name>**

Screen-l is an academic discussion list for those involved in film and TV studies. Topics include film theory, criticism, history, production, and instructional issues.

> **Screenwriting Discussion List** (scrnwrit)
> To subscribe, send e-mail to: **listserv@tamvm1.tamu.edu**
> Type in the body of your e-mail message: **subscribe scrnwrit <your name>**

Screenwriting is a high-volume forum for those interested in writing for TV or the big screen. Newbies and wannabes are welcome. There are a lot of good writing and market tips, and there's no shortage of emotional encouragement either.

Technical Writing

> **Technical Writing** (techwr-l)
> To subscribe, send e-mail to: **listserv@listserv.okstate.edu**
> Type in the body of your e-mail message: **subscribe techwr-l <your name>**

This is a discussion forum for technical writers and editors.

The Writing Life: Workshops and E-Mail Chats

The following lists are dedicated to the discussion of the writing life. Some, like Cyber-Sisters and WritersChat, function as discussion forums about the artist's way. Others, like Writers and the Writing Workshop, function as high-traffic e-mail workshops whose members routinely submit works in progress for critiquing.

These grassroots e-mail workshops are great places to meet fellow writers and polish your craft among peers. For more on grassroots workshops that are held in live chat rooms, rather then via e-mail, see Chapter 9, "The Online Writery: Real-Time Chats, Workshops, and Academic Writing Resources," which is about online writeries. For information on accredited college and university certificate and degree programs offered online, see Chapter 2, "Learning Vital New Skills: Virtual Universities and Training Institutes," on virtual universities.

The Artist's Way
To subscribe, send e-mail to: **listserver@waterw.com**
Type in the body of your e-mail message: **subscribe aw**
http://www.waterw.com/~lucia/aw.html

The Artist's Way, a book by Julia Cameron, outlines a twelve-step regime for artists wanting to get in touch with their creative processes. The Artist's Way list invites authors to join the twelve-step recovery-style program to gain support from others who are following the same path to creative recovery.

Black on White (BOW)
To subscribe, send e-mail to: **majordomo@mail.li.com**
Type in the body of your e-mail message: **subscribe bowlist**
http://www1.minn.net/~haartman/welcome.html

The Black on White list is a writers' forum that provides information and inspiration on how to overcome writer's block and creative procrastination.

Cyber-Sisters
To subscribe, send e-mail to: **majordomo@cgim.com**
Type in the body of your e-mail message: **subscribe cyber-sisters**
http://www.cybergrrl.com/cybersisters

Cyber-Sisters is a discussion forum for women artists.

Erotic Workshop
To subscribe, send e-mail to: **mohanraj@mills.edu**
Type in the subject of your e-mail message: **request erotica workshop info**

Erotic is a workshop for writers of erotica.

Fantasy Writers (fw)
To subscribe, send e-mail to: **listserv@maelstrom.stjohns.edu**
Type in the body of your e-mail message: **subscribe fw <your name>**

Fantasy Writers is a workshop open to all fantasy authors.

Journal Keeping
To subscribe, send e-mail to: **majordomo@goonsquad.spies.com**
Type in the body of your e-mail message: **subscribe journals**

Journal keeping is a discussion forum for those who keep journals or diaries as personal chronicles and exercises in creativity.

Science Fiction & Fantasy Critique (sfnf-critique)
To subscribe, send e-mail to: **majordomo@seidel.ncsa.uiuc.edu**
Type in the body of your e-mail message: **subscribe sfnf-critique**
<your name>
http://seidel.ncsa.uiuc.edu/SFnF-Writers/Default.html

Sfnf is a writers' workshop. Members submit works in progress for critique by other list members. The Web site houses biographies of list members as well as an archive of works submitted for critiquing.

SFNovelist
To subscribe, send e-mail to: **victory@crayne.com**
Type in the body of your e-mail message: a human-readable message about your background and why you wish to join the list
http://www.webcom.com/~victory/sfnovel.html

Victory Crayne moderates this list for writers working on hard science novels in the science fiction genre. Hard science novels are those that use a believable science basis. Members submit works for critique and agree in exchange to critique the works of fellow members.

Writers
To subscribe, send e-mail to: **listserv@mitvma.mit.edu**
Type in the body of your e-mail message: **subscribe writers <your name>**

Writers is a high-volume writers' workshop and chat session. If you're looking for community to help you hammer out your works, drop in on this list. This list caters largely to short fiction and poetry writers, though nonfiction is sometimes critiqued.

Writers—Creative Writers
To subscribe, send e-mail to: **listserv@wvnvm.wvnet.edu**
Type in the body of your e-mail message: **subscribe writers <your name>**

A general discussion list for creative and fiction writers.

Writer's Internet Exchange (write)
To subscribe, send e-mail to: **jkent@ilinks.net**
Type in the body of your e-mail message: a human-readable short bio on your writing background and your reasons for wanting to join the list.
http://www.ilinks.net/~jkent/write/

Janet Kent moderates this private list. Write is open by subscription to advanced or published writers seeking to polish their work. Members are admitted on a space-available basis and must agree to contribute at least three times each month to the ongoing critique of the work of others or by presentation of original work.

The Writing Workshop
To subscribe, send e-mail to: **listserv@psuvm.psu.edu**
Type in the body of your e-mail message: **subscribe writing <your name>**

The Writing Workshop is a series of online writing conferences. If you're just learning to write, or you need sound feedback on where your writing goes awry, drop in on these lists. Separate lists are maintained for different types of writing, as follows: Nfiction is the Non-Fiction Writers' Workshop; Fiction is the Fiction Writers' Workshop; Novels-L is the Novel Writers' Workshop; Poetry-W is the Poetry Writers' Workshop; Script-W is the Scriptwriters' Workshop; Writing is for general writing discussions; YAWrite is the Youth and Children Writers' Workshop. A subscribe message to **listserv@psuvm.psu.edu** will get you a welcome message on the different workshops in progress and how to join.

WritingChat (The Virtual Coffeshop)
To subscribe, send e-mail to: **majordomo@bel.avonibp.co.uk**
Type in the body of your e-mail message: **subscribe writingchat**

The Writing Chat is a cozy chat place for writers seeking to swap world views and news on the writing life.

WriteLab (The Writing Lab)
To subscribe, send e-mail to: **listserv@psuvm.psu.edu**
Type in the body of your e-mail message: **subscribe writelab <your name>**

Drop in here for writing exercises and critiques to keep your brain humming. All applicants are screened and held to a pledge to contribute and critique works at regular intervals. A set of writing exercises is given to all members.

> **#Writers Critique Lists**
> To subscribe, send e-mail to: the list-request address given below for each topic.
> Type in the subject of your e-mail message: **subscribe**
> **http://www.getset.com/writers/**

The # symbol (#Writers Critique Lists) is the symbol used before the name of an Internet Relay Chat (IRC) channel. This series of writers' discussion and critique lists is operated by the Undernet #writers online chat group. Available lists are as follows:

WritersTalk-request@niestu.com (general discussion)

RomanceCrit-request@niestu.com (romance)

FreelanceCrit-request@niestu.com (freelancers)

InspirationCrit-request@niestu.com (religious)

Mystery-Crit@request@niestu.com (mystery)

FictionCrit@request@niestu.com (contemporary fiction)

ShortsCrit@request@niestu.com (short stories)

SpecFicCrit@request@niestu.com (science fiction/ horror/fantasy)

Electronic Newsletters

While mailing lists are interactive, allowing you to post e-mail messages to the list to form a chain of conversation, electronic newsletters arrive quietly once or twice a month in your e-mail box. They do not offer an interactive feature. You cannot post your own messages to them. The following Writers' electronic newsletters dish out information on writing for the markets as well as new Net resources.

Directory of Writing-Related Newsletters

@Writers
To subscribe, send e-mail to: **majordomo@samurai.com**
Type in the body of your e-mail message: **subscribe a-writers**
http://www.geocities.com/Athens/Acropolis/6608

"@Writers" is a newsletter featuring market, resource, and how-to information for writers in all markets and genres. Back issues are archived online.

Inklings
To subscribe, send e-mail to: **majordomo@samurai.com**
Type in the body of your e-mail message: **subscribe inklings**
http://www.inkspot.com/

"Inklings" is an informational newsletter for writers of all stripes. The twice-monthly newsletter features columns on poetry, children's, mystery, horror, and romance markets. A Fresh Ink section highlights new Net resources for writers. Back issues are archived online.

WordSmith: A Word a Day
http://www.wordsmith.org/awad/awad.html
To subscribe, send e-mail to: **wsmith@wordsmith.org**
Type in the subject line of your e-mail: **subscribe <your name>**

A Word a Day is a fun, free service that delivers a new vocabulary word to your e-mail address every day.

The Writer's Page
To subscribe, send e-mail to: **WritersPage-request@niestu.com**
Type in the subject line your e-mail message: **subscribe**
http://www.getset.com/writers

This newsletter from the Undernet IRC group of writers is especially helpful for those interested in learning more about Internet Relay Chat conferences and workshops online. Stories, poetry, kudos, new book releases, and market information are featured in the newsletter.

CHAPTER 2

Learning Vital New Skills:
Virtual Universities and Training Institutes

There is no magic road to becoming a successful writer. No blueprint to instant success. Perpetual learning is the hallmark of the professional writer. Earning a college degree will not make you a writer. Earning a professional credential will not make you a writer. The only way you can become a writer is to write. And write. (Scary thought, eh?)

Most inveterate writers work alone, freelancing through life on a project-by-project basis. Most who succeed commercially—meaning that they pay their way with their writing money—practice more than one type of writing or diversify the markets they write for as time passes.

While the public enjoys the notion that writers are born prodigies, writers know that they must painstakingly forge themselves. Over and over again. Writers are not surprised to learn that it took T. S. Eliot seven years, and a great deal of seemingly idle study and creative incubation, to write his one hallmark poem, "Waste Land."

Perhaps more than any other profession, that of a writer requires relentless learning and relearning. Writers are communicators. Not a few of us communicate "how-to" install the latest software by day, while communicating the poetic mysteries of the human heart by night.

Given the nature of writing—as a solitary undertaking, one that increasingly occurs in front of a blinking box with a modem at the heart of its own amazing communication capabilities—it stands to reason that as colleges spring up along the Information Superhighway, writers will be among the first to take a seat inside these new electronic lecture halls.

Distance Learning Today

American colleges and universities have offered learners the chance to study independently, at home, since the previous century. It is now possible to take more than 14,000 courses from about 600 accredited institutions through home study. In 1996, an estimated 4 million Americans registered for self-study, many of them enrolling in computer- or Internet-assisted courses.

One thing new about independent correspondence study today is that learners are no longer limited to studying TV repair or court reporting. The universities that are online today are not the same ones that two decades ago caught the public eye, if for no other reason than the oddity of the notion that completing the coupon inside a matchbook cover could lead to learning how to drive a diesel truck.

The historically heavy emphasis on vocational training via correspondence, and the stigma associated with the way that process promoted itself in the United States, is being replaced by a new kind of home study: computer-assisted distance learning. Today, writers can study under the tutelage of a New York–based novelist or a Los Angeles–based Academy Award–winning scriptwriter without ever leaving the place most writers cherish the most—their computer keyboards.

How Distance Learning Works

Historically, independent study worked by having learners follow a written textbook and structured syllabus. Just like on campus, learners received a syllabus of course goals and objectives and weekly reading assignments. Each week, written assignments were turned in through surface mail to faculty for marking.

Exams were taken under the watchful eye of a proctor at a local college or library.

This basic method of self-study worked well for more than a century, but it also meant that it might take three weeks to get a question answered or an assignment returned. If you were really stumped, there was no chance to get protracted attention or help at a distance. You couldn't pass notes in class to solicit input from your classmates. You were, in many ways, on your own.

E-Mail: The Hermes of Distance Learning

With the advent of e-mail, it is possible to pose a question to an instructor and receive a response on the very same day—even in the very same hour. The cousin of e-mail, mailing lists, allow geographically distant learners to engage in e-mail banter back and forth, forming a collective discussion of any issue from the use of symbolism in the works of James Joyce to what's wrong with Billy Bob's short story (which everyone has received in a text file via e-mail and has dutifully read, *right?*). E-mail is the easiest Internet tool to access and master. Accordingly, distance-learning colleges are adopting e-mail at a dizzying rate.

If you've been thinking that a Master of Fine Arts would enhance your income through teaching engagements, you'll want to drop in at Goddard College in Vermont. Goddard, a fully accredited, yet nontraditional learning center, caters to creative types. Aspiring writers visit campus for only two to three weeks each year. Learners are assigned personal writing mentors, then remain connected to their mentors and fellow learners via e-mail as they work off-campus on self-selected creative projects.

Need some background study to launch your career as a mystery writer? The University of Minnesota's e-mail-assisted course, Ellery Queen and the American Detective Novel, may provide the inspiration that you seek.

Finally, if you've finished that screenplay and want an experienced assessment of what you've really created, the UCLA Writer's Program will assign your work to an experienced screenwriter for a detailed critique—via e-mail of course.

The World Wide Web: The Hercules of Distance Learning

One of the best developed Web-based campuses is administered by the nonprofit organization Spectrum Virtual University. Tens of thousands of people with Net access attend Spectrum's self-guided online tutorials each semester. Spectrum, the world's first free online college, offers courses to a worldwide audience. Spectrum's well-developed campus and interesting array of courses make it a must see if you are interested in learning or teaching in cyberspace. (Volunteer instructors are actively recruited in the arts and creative fields, by the way.)

At Spectrum, each week's lesson is stored on a Web page for weekly reading and review. Visiting Spectrum's Web site is not unlike going to the reference desk at a college library to check out a reserve reading. Electronic bulletin boards, embedded in Spectrum's Web pages, allow learners to drop in, post comments on their weekly assignments, and chat with classmates from Athabasca to Aberdeen.

Electronic Group Conferencing: The Roman Forum of Distance Learning

Colleges are only beginning to use the Net to deliver courses and workshops of interest to writers. Many independent study courses remain print based, simply adding e-mail to send lessons or query faculty. Programs such as UCLA's Writer's Program are experimenting with the use of online bulletin boards where learners can post questions and engage in classroom banter and debate. Each UCLA class also holds an optional live weekly lecture and discussion online, using Internet Relay Chat (IRC). IRC, as covered in Chapter 9, "The Online Writery: Real-Time Chats, Workshops, and Academic Writing Resources," allows writers to congregate online in real time to discuss weekly assignments.

Much of what is happening for writers using online conferencing and chat software is covered in detail in Chapter 9, on online writeries. Refer to that chapter particularly if you are interested in grassroots, noncollegiate mentoring using online means.

Virtual Colleges and Universities: A Resource Directory

Some of the programs listed below offer degrees through distance study with little or no time spent on campus. Most of the programs offer courses that award degree credits that can be used to meet graduate school prerequisites in writing or literature or applied toward a degree at your local college.

All of the following schools offer writers a chance to learn new-market writing skills, such as multimedia instructional design, screenwriting, Web page publishing, or technical writing.

If college degree credits are awarded for course completion, the number of credits awarded for each course is indicated in parentheses following the course title. Unless otherwise indicated, academic credits are awarded in traditional semester units. Course titles listed reflect the offerings at the time this guide went to print. Course titles and offerings will vary from semester to semester. E-mail the colleges directly or visit their sites on the World Wide Web for current information on course and degree offerings.

> **City University**
> Distance Learning Admissions
> 919 S.W. Grady Way
> Renton, WA 98055
> 206-624-1688
> 800-422-4898
> E-Mail: **info@cityu.edu**
> **http://www.cityu.edu**

City is a private college, founded in the 1970s to serve the escalating number of adult and mid-career learners. A variety of bachelor's and master's degrees may be earned through distance learning with no campus visits. Undergraduate Bachelor of Arts degrees are available with writing concentrations in Literature and Comparative Literature, or Mass Communications and Journalism. Full programs are also offered on campus in Washington State. Only selected courses support e-mail lesson options. Others use surface mail and FAX options. Individual courses are open to enrollment by non-degree learners. Tuition averages $184 per upper level undergraduate quarter credit or $920 per course.

Literature and Comparative Literature Concentration

> Literature of Antiquity (5)
> Literature of the Middle Ages (5)

Literature of the Renaissance (5)

Shakespeare: Comedies (5)

Shakespeare: Tragedies (5)

Literature of the Enlightenment (5)

Literature of the Romantic Age (5)

European Literature of the Nineteenth Century (5)

European Literature of the Twentieth Century (5)

Literature and Technology (5)

Central European Literature (5)

American Literature of the Colonial and Federal Periods (5)

Nineteenth Century American Literature (5)

Twentieth Century American Literature (5)

Contemporary American Literature (5)

Mass Communications and Journalism Concentration

Journalistic Writing (5)

Legal and Ethical Issues in Communications (5)

Communications and Public Relations (5)

Visual/Photo Communications (5)

Electoral Politics and Mass Media (5)

History of Mass Communications in the United States (5)

Broadcast Script and News Writing (5)

Goddard College
Off-Campus Programs
Plainfield, VT 05667
802-454-8311
800-468-4888
E-Mail: **admissions@earth.goddard.edu**
http://www.goddard.edu/

Goddard supports low-residency bachelor's and master's degrees for independent learners. A self-designed Bachelor of Arts in Media and Communications, Master of Arts, Master of Fine Arts, or the Masters in Expressive Arts in Education may be earned through Goddard.

Learners and faculty mentors at Goddard communicate through surface mail and e-mail. Degree-seekers must attend one- to two-week residencies on campus, twice each year. Learners work with faculty to design their own degree programs and learning contracts. Goddard allows professionally established artists who do not hold traditional academic credentials to petition into graduate-level study. Tuition averages $3,498 per semester (undergraduate); $4,028 per semester (graduate).

New Jersey Institute of Technology
Continuing and Professional Education
Guttenberg Information Technologies, 5th Floor
University Heights
Newark, NJ 07102-1982
973-596-3060
800-624-9850
E-Mail: **dl@njit.edu**
http://www.njit.edu/cpe

The New Jersey Institute of Technology is a public college. Graduate-level distance learning courses are delivered via mailed videotapes of on-campus lectures, with e-mail lesson submission. FAX and voice mail are also used to communicate with faculty. Certificates are also offered in several computer technologies areas. Tuition averages $326 per credit (New Jersey); $451 per credit (Others).

Graduate Certificate in Practice of Technical Communications

Advanced Professional and Technical Communications (3)

Document Design and Desktop Publishing (3)

Proposal Writing (3)

Collaborative and Interpersonal Communications (3)

New School for Social Research
Distance Instruction for Adult Learners
66 West 12th Street
New York, NY 10011
212-229-5880
E-Mail: **dialexec@dialnsa.edu**
http://www.dialnsa.edu

Those who know New York City know the New School, located in Greenwich Village, as an historical haven for Europeans who thought, wrote, or created left of center earlier in this century. The New School's DIAL (Distance Instruction for Adult Learners) program has made the Greenwich Village cafe culture another stop on your modem strings. Applicants need access to the New School's virtual campus on the World Wide Web as well as basic e-mail capabilities.

Classes meet online for nine weeks each semester. Most courses award three semester credits. Learners may also register in courses on a noncredit basis. Applicants can complete a Bachelor of Arts degree completely online. Tuition averages $512 per credit; $320–$405 per non-credit course.

Literature

Technology in Literature and Film (3)

William Blake and the Poetics of Revolutionary Vision (3)

The Bronte Sisters (3)

Writing Women's Lives (3)

The Empire Writes Back: Post-Colonial Literature (3)

Emerson, Whitman, and Thoreau (3)

Literature of the Harlem Renaissance (3)

Post-Stonewall Gay Drama (3)

Contemporary Aesthetics (3)

How to Read a Platonic Dialogue (3)

Women in French Literature and Film (French) (3)

Contemporary Latin American Short Stories (3)

Writing

Opening the Imagination: A Prose Poetry Workshop (3)

Advanced Poetry Workshop (3)

Beginning Fiction Workshop (3)

Fiction Writing Workshop (3)

Fiction Writing, Memory, Imagination, Desires (3)

The Great American Short Story (3)

Intermediate Fiction Workshop: The Poetry of Fact and How to Write It (3)

Multigenre Writing: From Roots, Recall, Research (3)

Reading for Writing (3)

Writer's Workout: A Workshop for Intensive Critique (3)

A Subject of One's Own: Fiction and Nonfiction (3)

Foregrounding the Wild: An Advanced Workshop for All Genres (3)

Hypertext Poetry and Fiction (3)

Theater Criticism (3)

Jazz Writing (3)

Screenwriting 1 (3)

Screenwriting 2 (3)

Writing for Magazines (3)

Playwriting (3)

New York Institute of Technology
Online Campus
P.O. Box 9029
Central Islip, NY 11722-9029
516-686-7712
800-222-6948
E-Mail: **mlehmann@acl.nyit.edu** (Maggie Lehman)
http://sunp.nyit.edu/olc/

The New York Institute of Technology (NYIT) is a private university. The NYIT Online Campus is one of the first completely online degree programs in the

United States. All courses are offered with an e-mail lesson option and online conferencing where learners meet, post questions, and participate in course discussions.

A Bachelor of Arts, Science, or Professional Studies, with concentrations in English, Humanities, Technical Writing, and several other areas, may be earned completely online. Tuition averages $200 per credit.

Writing and Literature

Introduction to Journalism (3)

Basic Reading and Writing (3)

Basic Reading and Writing for International Students (3)

College Composition I (3)

College Composition II (3)

Business Writing (3)

Technical Writing (3)

Report Writing (3)

Advanced Scientific and Technical Writing (3)

Advanced Writing and Editing Techniques (3)

The Art of Drama (3)

The Art of Prose: Scientific and Technical Writing (3)

The Art of Fiction (3)

Internship in Professional Writing (3)

Shakespeare (3)

Literature Seminar (3)

UCLA Extension
Writer's Online Program
10995 Le Conte Avenue
Los Angeles, CA 90024-2883
310-825-9416
800-784-8436
E-Mail: **writers@unex.ucla.edu**
http://www.unex.ucla.edu/On_line.htm

The UCLA (University of California Los Angeles) Extension supports the largest continuing-education program for writers in the United States. The on-campus program offers more than 450 courses in all areas of writing, from comic books to interactive game scripting. The distance online program boasts an impressive array of alumni and faculty. Recent alumni include the screenwriters for *Mrs. Doubtfire* and *Grumpy Old Men*.

The Writer's Program launched an "electronic classroom" option in 1995. The online program intends to add more courses each semester depending on demand. Instruction takes place through the weekly exchange of e-mail with instructors and fellow students. Students have the option of attending class once a week online using an IRC (Internet Relay Chat) program. Average cost for a three-credit course is $385–$485.

Writers with completed manuscripts may submit their work to the faculty of the Writer's Program. Critiques and consultations may occur by e-mail for those not able to attend a conference in Los Angeles. The fee structure for a Writing Consultation is published below.

Writer's Professional Consultations

Novels: $950

Nonfiction Books: $700

Screenplays: $700

TV Script: $500

Per Hour: $90

Writing

Business Writing: An Online Tutorial (3)

Creating the Scene (3)

Creativity into Craft: A Workshop in Fiction Writing (3)

Introduction to Comedy Writing for TV and Film (3)

Introduction to Fiction: Learning the Fundamentals (2)

Introduction to Screenwriting (3)

Introduction to Screenwriting II (3)

Screenwriting III: Finishing the Script (3)

Introduction to Short Story Writing (3)

The Short Story: An Online Writing Workshop (3)

Story Structures for Interactive Software (3)

Technical Writing: An Online Tutorial (3)

Technology-Based Fiction (3)

Writing the First Novel: An Online Workshop (3)

Writing Nonfiction for Publication (3)

Writing from Reading (3)

Writing the Sitcom (3)

University of Iowa
Center for Credit Programs
116 International Center
Iowa City, IA 52242-1802
319-335-2575
800-272-6430
E-Mail: **credit-programs@uiowa.edu**
http://gcs.ccp.uiowa.edu

The University of Iowa offers more than 160 college courses through correspondence. A no-residency Bachelor of Liberal Studies degree may also be earned through Iowa's modestly priced distance learning program. Some writing course instructors are graduate teaching assistants in Iowa's renowned Graduate Writer's Workshop. The Iowa Writer's Workshop is considered one of the best academic writing schools for fiction in the United States. Learners may submit their lessons via e-mail, but not all instructors reply via e-mail. Some courses may be taken for graduate credit. Tuition averages $77 per semester credit.

Writing

Advanced Playwriting (3)

Creative Writing (3)

Nonfiction Writing (3)

Fiction Writing (Advanced Fiction Writing) (3)

Fiction Writing (Advanced Fiction Writing II) (3)

Free-Lance Reporting and Writing (3)

Section 1: Poetry Writing (3)

Section 2: Poetry Writing (Advanced Poetry Writing) (3)

Section 1: Screenwriting (3)

Section 2: Screenwriting (Advanced) (3)

Writing for Practical Purposes (3)

Nonfiction Writing (3)

Literature

Selected American Works (3)

Shakespeare (3)

Selected Authors (Major Nineteenth-Century British Works) (3)

Literature and Culture of Twentieth-Century America (3)

Chaucer (3)

English Novel: Scott to Butler (3)

Popular Literature (Detective Fiction) (3)

Regional Women Writers (Southern Women Writers) (3)

Women in Literature (Representative Women Writers) (3)

Changing Concepts of Women in Literature (3)

Literature and Philosophical Thought (The Holocaust) (3)

Science Fiction (Historical Survey) (3)

Prose by Women Writers (Feminist Fiction) (3)

The Interpretation of Literature (3)

Literatures of the African People (3)

University of Maryland
Bachelor's Degree-at-a-Distance
University Boulevard at Adelphi Road
College Park, MD 20742-1660
301-985-7000
800-283-6832
E-Mail: **umucinfo@nova.umuc.edu**
http://www.umuc.edu/distance/

The University of Maryland has offered Bachelor's degrees through distance learning for more than two decades. Tycho, the University of Maryland's graphically oriented software, allows Net-connected learners to correspond with instructors, receive online career and educational advice, obtain tutoring, and access computer-based multimedia courseware. Most courses also allow for the use of voice mail for learners to "speak" with instructors. Some, but not all, courses are offered with e-mail or online-conferencing options each semester. Degree majors of interest to writers include Communication Studies (English and Business Communication) and the Humanities. Individual courses are open to nondegree learners. Tuition averages $176 per credit (Maryland); $203 per credit (Others).

English and Communication

Introduction to Writing (3)

Studies in Fiction, Poetry, and Drama (3)

English and American Literature: Blake to Conrad (3)

Twentieth Century African-American Literature: The Fictional Vision (3)

Critical Analysis in Reading and Writing (3)

Shakespeare: Power and Justice (3)

Writing for Managers (3)

University of Minnesota
Department of Independent Study
45 Wesbrook Hall
77 Pleasant Street SE
Minneapolis, MN 55455
612-624-0000
800-234-6564
E-Mail: **indstudy@ tc.umn.edu**
http://www.cee.umn.edu/dis

The University of Minnesota offers one of the largest undergraduate distance course programs in the United States. Of Minnesota's 200-plus courses, many of them in Literature, Foreign Languages, or the Humanities, more than 90 of them allow for e-mail lesson submission. The program intends to increase offerings of e-mail and Web-based courses in the coming years. A certificate in organizational and professional communication may be earned via the Internet. Below is a sample of distance course offerings with e-mail options. Costs average $95.50 per quarter credit.

Literature

Afro-American Literature (4)

Asian American Literature (4)

Introduction to African Literature (4)

Ellery Queen: The American Detective Story (4)

Russian Literature: Middle Ages to Dostoevsky (4)

Selections from Latin Literature (4)

Writing

Magazine Writing (4)

Writing in the Social Sciences (4)

Writing About Literature (4)

Writing About Science (4)

Writing for the Arts (4)

Technical Writing for Engineers (4)

Intermediate Fiction Writing (4)

Intermediate Poetry Writing (4)

Topics in Creative Writing (4)

Electronic and Print Based Document Design (4)

Introduction to Computer-Based Instructional Design (MAC Authorware) (4)

Grant Proposal Writing (3)

University of Nebraska
Department of Distance Education
Division of Continuing Studies
Clifford Hardin Nebraska Center for Continuing Education
Room 336
33rd & Holdrege Streets
Lincoln, NE 68583-9800
402-472-4321
E-Mail: **unldde@unl.edu**
http://www.unl.edu:80/conted/disted/index.html

The University of Nebraska has offered independent-study courses since 1909. More than 85 courses are offered in professional and liberal arts areas at the undergraduate level. All Nebraska independent-study courses support an e-mail lesson option. Semester credits are awarded. Tuition averages $85 per credit.

Broadcasting

Introduction to Broadcasting (3)

Broadcast Writing (3)

Advanced Broadcast Writing (3)

English and Literature

Composition I (3)

Twentieth-Century Fiction (3)

Shakespeare (3)

Composition (Intermediate) (3)

Business Writing (3)

Special Topics in Writing (3)

Scientific Greek and Latin (3)

University of Washington
Extension Division
Independent Study
Box 354223
5001 25th Avenue, NE
Seattle, WA 98105
206-543-2320
800-543-2320
E-Mail: **distance@u.washington.edu**
http://weber.u.washington.edu/~distance/

The University of Washington Independent Study program offers a variety of undergraduate courses as well as a special noncredit Certificate in Literary Fiction. A 27-credit Certificate in School Library Media is valid for learners seeking K–12 school certification in Alaska and Washington State. Two summer sessions are required on campus for that program.

Learners may submit assignments via e-mail, pose questions to their instructors via e-mail, and gain access to the university's general library and resource systems while online. Tuition averages $74 per quarter credit. Noncredit courses average $315 each.

Certificate in Literary Fiction

Introduction to Literary Fiction Writing (0)

Intermediate Literary Writing (0)

Advanced Literary Writing (0)

Literature

Reading Literature (5)

The Bible as Literature (5)

World Literature and Culture (5)

Shakespeare (5)

Reading Fiction (5)

Shakespeare to 1603 (5)

Shakespeare after 1603 (5)

English Literature: The Late Renaissance (5)

Milton (5)

The Modern Novel (5)

Fantasy (5)

English Novel: Early and Middle 19th Century (5)

American Literature: The Early Modern Period (5)

American Literature: Contemporary (5)

Children's Literature (5)

Writing

Composition: Exposition (5)

Introduction to Technical Writing (3)

Style in Scientific and Technical Writing (3)

Intermediate Expository Writing (5)

Advanced Expository Writing (5)

Advanced Seminar: Verse Writing (5)

Beginning Short Story Writing (5)

Advanced Seminar: Verse (Poetry) Writing (5)

Intermediate Seminar: Verse (Poetry) Writing (5)

Intermediate Seminar: Short Story Writing (5)

Communications and Media

History and Development of Communication and Journalism (5)

Mass Media Law (5)

Women, Minorities, and Media (5)

USDA Graduate School
Correspondence Program
Stop 9911
Room 1112 South
1400 Independence Avenue, S.W.
Washington, D.C. 20250-9911
202-720-7123
E-Mail: **correspond@grad.usda.gov**
http://grad.usda.gov/corres/corpro.html

The USDA (United States Department of Agriculture) Graduate School has sponsored professional study programs since 1921. More than 50,000 learners study through the USDA's programs each year, both on campus and through correspondence. While the USDA School is not an accredited degree-granting college, most of its courses and programs have been reviewed by the American Council on Education (ACE) and judged to be the equivalent of courses offered by regionally accredited colleges. Courses are fully acceptable for promotion and salary grade increases within United States government agencies.

The On-Line Education (OLE) program allows learners to submit assignments via e-mail and participate in learning activities via access to a Bulletin Board Service (BBS). The professional Certificates in Editing are designed for those preparing for careers as book editors, magazine editors, technical documentation writers, and newsletter or product information editors. Tuition averages $210–$350 per course, including textbooks.

Certificate of Accomplishment in Editorial Practices

Introduction to the Editing Process (3)
Intermediate Editing (3)
Printing, Layout, and Design (3)
Advanced Practice in Editing (3)

Certificate of Accomplishment in Technical Editorial Practices

Introduction to the Editing Process (3)

Printing, Layout, and Design (3)

Technical Editing (3)

Plus one elective:

Intermediate Editing (3)

Basic Indexing (3)

Applied Indexing (3)

Legal Writing (3)

Introduction to On-Line Communication (2)

Introduction to Visual Communication (2)

Certificate of Accomplishment in Editorial Management

Successful completion of the above two Certificates

Plus two required courses:

Information and Records Management (2)

Publishing Management (3)

Certificate of Accomplishment in Library Techniques

Successful completion of five core courses:

Introduction to Library Techniques (2)

Descriptive Cataloging (3)

Subject Cataloging and Classification (2)

Basic Reference Service and Reference Tools (1)

Introduction to Bibliographies (2)

Plus at least seven credits of electives:

Library Media Services (2)

Use of Archives and Manuscripts (2)

Legal Literature (3)

Introduction to the Editing Process (3)

Basic Indexing (3)

Introduction to On-Line Communication (2)

Introduction to Information Systems Technology (2)

Report Writing (1)

Private Educational Enterprises

Spectrum Virtual University
E-Mail: **handbook@vu.org**
http://www.vu.org

Spectrum Virtual University is the world's first free online college. Spectrum isn't a university in the orthodox sense of the word. No degrees are offered and no college credits are awarded. The teaching staff is strictly volunteer. Many courses are self-guided tutorials, with little instructor feedback.

Yet, Spectrum is tuition-free, and it offers an impressive array of courses in the creative arts as well as culturally intriguing topics. We highly recommend a visit to this online campus. It is likely that the virtual universities of the future will take strong cues from Spectrum's innovative use of mailing lists, e-mail, bulletin boards, and lesson-archiving systems. Spectrum's courses on exploring the World Wide Web and the Internet are great places to learn how to really cruise cyberspace, hands-on.

Exploring the Internet

Exploring the World Wide Web

Eight Weeks to Creative Writing

Mystical Traditions in Literature

Writers on the Net
E-Mail: **writers@writers.com**
http://www.writers.com/

Writers on the Net is a cooperative of published authors and teachers who provide writing workshops, tutoring, and mentoring online. Courses are offered via e-mail, with a mailing-list format used to simulate class discussion and critiques. Class availability may differ from time to time, but courses are commonly offered in the areas listed below. Classes typically last six to ten weeks. Fees range from $50 to $240

Writing Dark Fantasy and Horror

Writing the Science Fiction Novel

Scriptwriting—Screen and Stage

Writing and Publishing Magazine Articles

How to Write and Sell a Contemporary Romance Novel

Literary Fiction Writing

Getting that Novel Started

Poetry Writing

Short Story Writing

Writing for Interactive Media

Hypertext 101 for Writers

Mystery, Thriller, and Suspense Writing

Writing for the Stand-Up Comedian

Ziff-Davis University (ZDU)
http://www.zdu.com
eZone
http://www.waite.com/ezone

Ziff-Davis's ZDU and Waite Press's eZone are examples of desktop training universities built by publishers who are taking their tutorial-style books and tying them to automated self-study modules on the Web. For a low monthly subscription fee, learners can access online-learning modules. Working through the automated tutorials allows learners to quickly master new technical and computer-related skills, like HTML 3 and Java Programming, for Web publishing.

Keeping Current with Online Learning

Adult Education & Distance Learner's Resource Center
E-Mail: **LifeLearn@aol.com**
http://www.together.net/~lifelong

This center, developed and maintained by the authors of this guide, contains a collection of annotated links to the best virtual colleges and training sites on the Net, and a growing collection of helpful articles about how to locate and attend an accredited virtual university or training institute.

Globewide Network Academy
E-Mail: **gna@uu-gna.mit.edu**
http://www.gnacademy.org/

The Globewide Network Academy (GNA) online catalog lists distance-learning courses from colleges, training institutes, and independent workshop providers of all stripes. Several noncredit writing and creative arts courses are listed with GNA. Offerings will vary, as will course fees and tuition. Anyone can list courses here.

Electrifying Your Career:
Online and Freelance Writing Opportunities

If you've written for print publications, you may be considering writing for the online or computer markets. If so, you'll find no shortage of places to freelance or market your work online. This chapter outlines career trends for cyberscribes and provides an annotated directory to the best freelancing sites and media job boards online.

If you have a strong interest in technology and how computers work, there is a vast market on the Internet for technical writers—authors who research and write materials like computer manuals and engineering instructional units. Many of the super job posting sites on the World Wide Web discussed in this chapter, like the Monster Board, are heavy in postings for freelance or staff technical writers who are experienced in specialized computer systems or languages.

But you don't have to be a techno-geek to write for online markets. We often write human interest features about cyberlife—articles about how real people are using the Net to communicate and socialize. The emphasis here is not on the technology but on social trends and events. Even the most technologically challenged writers are capable of writing these kinds of human interest stories for online or traditional print publications. As the Net becomes integrated into the fabric of American life, the market for human interest stories should keep expanding.

If you're uncertain as to what kind of cyberwriting might suit you, take the free Cyberscribes Career Classifier test online. The test is housed at Ellipsys International Publications <http://www.ellipsys.com> as a creative promotion for the book by Anne Hart, *Cyberscribes 1: The New Journalists*. The test will give you a helpful read on the kind of new media writing that might best suit your personality. Sample essays from *Cyberscribes 1* are posted to the Web site also. Take a peek at these essays to find out what industry experts and editors themselves envision as the best new career options for well-wired writers.

In today's Web publishing market, you should have no difficulty marketing yourself as a cyberscribe, especially if you have skills in hypertext mark-up language (HTML), which is a simple programming or tagging language. A knowledge of HTML will allow you to convert your text into interactive pages that can be posted to the Web. (For more information on HTML, see Chapter 15, "Browsing the World Wide Web.")

If you don't already have HTML skills, they aren't so difficult to acquire. Several online classes exist that teach HTML step by step. Writers On the Net offers such a class. So too do some of the virtual university programs reviewed in this book. If you want to learn how to write for the multimedia or technical markets, you can get these kinds of career-expanding courses and tutorials delivered over the Net, literally to your desktop.

Writers who author in text, then convert it to HTML for posting to the Web, are usually called *content creators* or *content authors*. To learn about HTML authoring and the world of online publishing, visit the home page of the HTML Writers Guild <http://www.hwg.org/>. The Guild supports an informative archive, mailing lists for HTML authors and designers, and a chat channel.

The advantage to knowing HTML, or having additional computer conversion skills, is that you can command a higher salary or freelance fees for your work. You will also find a much wider range of writing and editing assignments to choose from on the Net. We have done projects where we authored content for online resource centers and delivered the final product in text form for use as a final print publication, as well as in HTML form for use as online content. We charged two fees in these cases—one to research and write the material, the other a per-hour HTML formatting charge for the time it took to convert the written text to a Web posting format.

You don't have to be technically oriented or know HTML to write for some online markets, however. We author many educational lessons and articles the old-fashioned way—meaning we research and write them up on a word processor. We then e-mail the text to the company, magazine, or Web site that hired us.

No matter which markets you write for, there is one issue that should concern all writers these days. That issue is what to charge for the electronic use of one's articles or works across the Net or through a growing number of for-profit electronic redistribution databases like Lexis-Nexis and UnCover.

Copyrights and Electronic Rights

Do print magazines pay more for electronic rights to articles? If so, how much? If not, should they? What should you accept as a reasonable amount for the electronic licensing rights to your new book?

Authors face a plethora of legal issues brought about by the emerging industry known as e-publishing, or the creation of electronic books and texts. The Internet has been referred to as the world's largest copy machine. There's a great deal of truth in that statement. It is possible for anyone to copy your work and post it online for the world to read.

To stay sane, we've researched the issue of electronic rights and come up with some flexible industry standards. Much of what we have to say derives from the recommendations issued by the National Writer's Union, whose Web site and position papers can be freely accessed online.

First, as a freelance writer, remember that what you are selling is not an article; what you are selling is any number of publication rights to your article. The more rights editors seek to exploit, the more they should be willing to pay for your work. Traditionally, editors have sought and paid for first North American print serial rights. This means they are purchasing the right to be the first to publish your work in print form in the North American market.

The National Writer's Union recommends that all rights beyond first print rights be negotiated. Their recommendation is that freelancers ask for a fee of 15 percent more than was paid for print rights for the electronic rights. The 15 percent fee would entitle the publisher to archive an article online or in a database for a period of one year. Requests for longer archiving periods or wider electronic distribution rights, such as foreign syndication feeds or the right to sell your article as collective material in a CD-ROM format, should yield larger percentage fees.

Electronic or online storage rights for books are more complicated. Many authors and publishers see making parts of their books available for free on the Internet as a smart promotional move. For example, you can read the first two chapters of John Grisham's latest thriller for "free" in America Online's Book Notes section. But if you want to devour the whole book, you still have to buy it in print or hard copy form.

In an effort to help writers collect additional revenue from the growing unauthorized electronic use of their works in database and online resource centers, the National Writers Union (NWU), a trade union of more than 4,000 freelance authors, took two decisive actions. The first was a class action suit successfully brought on behalf of a group of freelance writers against the New York Times Company (*Tasini vs. The New York Times*).The second was to establish the Publication Rights Clearinghouse (PRC), a clearinghouse where writers can register their works for resale to the electronic and online markets. The NWU collects royalties and redistributes them directly to authors. UnCover, PRC's first licensee, is owned by Knight-Ridder and is the world's largest database distributor of journal, news, and magazine articles.

To assist writers in collecting royalties on the electronic use of their works by a burgeoning number of markets, the Author's Registry, an independent nonprofit organization, was born in 1995. Once a work is registered, the Registry collects electronic royalties from publishers, database producers, and reprint services, then regularly redistributes these royalties back to the author. Authors, agents, and publishers may register and participate. Currently, some of America's leading agencies, such as William Morris, and leading industry publishers, such as *Publisher's Weekly*, belong to the Registry.

Directory of Electronic Copyright Resources

American Society of Journalists & Authors (ASJA)—Contracts Watch
http://www.asja.org/

The ASJA, an organization for freelance journalists and writers, distributes "Contracts Watch." This electronic newsletter tattletales on publishers who are not paying their writers—or not paying them fairly. Legal actions pending over issues like copyright infringement and electronic rights are addressed. To receive "Contracts Watch," send the e-mail message "join asjacw-list" to <asja-manager@silverquick.com> with the words "contracts watch" in the e-mail subject header. Back issues and information on electronic rights are archived at the Web site.

Author's Registry
http://www.webcom.com/registry

A nonprofit clearinghouse that serves to collect and redistribute royalties to authors on the use of their works by the electronic markets. Literary agencies, individual authors, and publishers may register here to simplify the task of making payment for multiple electronic uses of original print productions.

CyBarrister Page
http://www.ssbb.com/cybarr.html

This page, from a law firm, chronicles how technology is way ahead of the law in terms of intellectual copyright protection. Details are given on the current state of the law and the use of works online on Web pages and in electronic databases.

Copyright & Fair Use Sight
http://fairuse.stanford.edu/

Stanford University's database on Internet copyright and intellectual property issues supports a keyword search for articles, test case summaries, and position papers on copyright law. This massive archive includes articles and links on copyright myths, multimedia rights, digital rights, and copyright abuse in computer and educational environments.

The Copyright Website
http://www.benedict.com/

This site archives articles on famous copyright infringement cases, copyright fundamentals, copyright registration, electronic copyright cases and disputes, and fair use and public domain laws.

National Writers Union & Publication Rights Clearinghouse
http://www.igc.apc.org/nwu/

The National Writers Union (NWU) Web site provides tips on negotiating electronic rights, what to do in cases of copyright infringement, sample contracts and clauses that have worked for other writers, and news summaries of the current efforts of freelancers to win payments for unauthorized electronic use of their work. Free vital publications that can be downloaded or ordered directly from the Web site include "Electronic Rights Guidelines for Journalists," "NWU Statement of Principles on Electronic Rights," and "Recommended Principles for Contracts Covering Online Book Publishing." Their 1995 survey *The Freelance Writers' Lot* is an eye-popping look at the low wages paid to freelance writers across markets.

United States Copyright Office
gopher://marvel.loc.gov/11/copyright

The government maintains this official gopher (see Chapter 16, "Finding and Retrieving Material on the Information Dirt Road: Telnet, FTP, Archie, Gopher, and Veronica") of articles on the copyright process. Information is housed here on applying for and protecting creative copyrights and on copyright resources on the Net.

Working Life: Jonathan Tasini's Home Page
http://www.Ira-ny.com/workinglife/index.html

Tasini, labor journalist and president of the National Writers Union, chronicles his fight to achieve fair working conditions and payment structures for freelance writers, including fees for electronic usage.

Freelancing Online: A How-To Primer

Composing Electronic Queries

If the publication you're interested in writing for accepts queries by e-mail rather than by surface mail, by all means take advantage of this fact and use e-mail to submit your query and your promotional clips. Why? Economics is a good answer. It's both less expensive and less time consuming to prepare and send a query via e-mail than it is by surface mail.

By the time you pay for paper, ink, postage, return postage, and copies of your clips, it costs about $3 for each serious query that you send by surface mail. If you query ten magazines for the same project using surface mail, you've spent $30 up front. Sending the same ten queries electronically costs next to nothing. The only expense is what you pay for your e-mail account.

Another benefit is that editors are much quicker to respond to e-mail queries than they are to surface mail queries. E-mail lands your query directly on the editor's desktop. All he or she needs to do is hit the reply key and type, "Sorry, not this time," or "Sounds good, let's try it." Chances are you'll receive a reply to an electronic query within the same week that you send it. Conversely, in our experience, you can wait months for a surface mail query to rise to the top of a paper slush pile and grab someone's attention.

Sending out follow-ups to your query letters is much easier using e-mail also. We keep a list of queries sent out in our e-mail "out" box. If we haven't heard back from an editor in two weeks, we hit the "send again" button and off goes our query again with a new note reminding the editor that we're still waiting to hear back.

Six Unbreakable Electronic Query Rules

1. **Craft Your Query with Care**   E-mail sometimes encourages people to write faster and with less thought. Don't make this mistake. Craft your electronic query letter as carefully as though it were going to be published.

2. **Spellcheck**   If your e-mail program does not have a spellcheck (many do not yet have this feature), compose your query in your regular word processing program, then save it as "text only" or an ASCII file, stripping it of all formatting. Spellcheck your query. Then copy the text and paste it into the body of your e-mail message.

3. **Send Your Query to a Person, Not a Publication**   Avoid sending e-mail to a general magazine address, like info@magazine.com. If you're not sure to whom you should e-mail your query, call the periodical and ask for the e-mail address of the editor who handles article queries. This is usually the managing editor. Use that person's e-mail address.

4. **Headline Your Query**   Use the header of your e-mail as you would a news headline. It's a good idea to mark your headers with the word "query" so an editor knows it is not junk mail. Then give your query a jazzy headline designed to catch an editor's weary eye.

5. **Include a Clip of Your Best Work**   Include a clip of your published work in the same e-mail that contains your query letter. One sample article as a clip at the end of your query will do. Avoid sending clips in attachment files to your e-mail because sending attached files is still a very uncertain business (see Item 6).

6. **Attach Text-Only Files**   Electronic files have to travel through many computer gateways before reaching their destinations. Attached files don't always make it to the other end uncorrupted. Unless you know what kind of computer and word-processing software the receiver has, never send attached e-mail that is formatted by a specific computer system or word-processing software. If you must send an attached file of your clips, strip your clips of all formatting and enhancements. Save your file as "text-only" or an ASCII file within your word processor. That way, your clip file can be easily opened and read by any system or software on the receiving end.

Master Directory of Freelancing Resources

Arachnoid Writer's Alliance
http://www.vena.com/arachnoid/about/marketing.html

The Arachnoid Alliance, based in Santa Cruz, California, bills itself as the world's first online independent writers' publishing coalition. Authors can upload sections of their unpublished or self-published novels or nonfiction tomes to the Library. Browsers can sample works and buy them directly from authors. Publishers and agents can browse the Library for new talent.

AuthorLink!
http://www.authorlink.com

AuthorLink! is an online repository that markets ready-to-publish works to agencies and acquisition editors. The site supports a browsable directory of manuscripts, both unpublished and self-published, that are available for representation. Book publishing news and informative interviews with agents are archived here also.

Computer Book Cafe—Studio B
http://www.studiob.com

The Computer Book Cafe, a project of Studio B, an agency specializing in computer books, archives articles of interest to freelance writers and those involved in computer book development. Informative articles include Steve O'Keefe's "Online Publicity for Authors" and Brian Gill's column, "Working Smart," which gives tips on contract negotiations. An Author's Spotlight section archives interviews with successful computer book authors. A work-for-hire service matches technical and computer writers and editors with clients for a percentage of the project fee.

Creative Freelancers Online
http://www.freelancers.com

Creative Freelancers, an employment agency in New York City, sponsors this site with registration and help-wanted ads for all types of creative freelancers. Architects, illustrators, photographers, authors, journalists, proofreaders, book designers, Web designers, musicians, scripters, computer artists, and editors may register here. Employers pay a commission when a successful match is made.

FAQ: Freelance Writing

This electronic FAQ (frequently asked questions) file by publicist and writer Marcia Yudkin is a good primer on the freelance writing life for those new to the business. It covers topics like, "Do you need an agent," and "How to deal with rejection letters." To receive a copy, send e-mail requesting a copy to the automatic reply function at <fl@yudkin.com>.

FAQ: How to Publish an Electronic Newsletter
http://www.inkspot.com/~ohi/ink/newsletterinfo.html

Authoring and distributing a free topic-specific monthly newsletter via e-mail can be a great way to promote yourself as an expert in any area. Debbie Ridpath Ohi, publisher of "Inklings," the largest free-circulation electronic newsletter for writers, archives this FAQ on how to create, distribute, and promote a periodic newsletter.

The Freelance Network
http://www.work4u.com/

Freelance writers can register their availability for contract work in the online database. Project directors can pick from 660 freelancers profiled in the database. Message board forums allow freelancers and project directors to network with each other. All types of freelancers and consultants register here, not just authors.

The Internet Writer's Guidelines Listing
http://wane5.scri.fsu.edu/~jtillman/DEV/ZDMS/

This database chronicles the submission guidelines and contact information for a host of primarily small, independent, nonpaying electronic magazines (e-zines) on the Net.

Oxbridge's Mediafinder
http://www.mediafinder.com

Oxbridge Communications has published printed media directories for more than twenty years. The MediaFinder is Oxbridge's master online directory to media—magazines, catalogs, newsletters and professional directories. The MediaFinder catalogs contact information on more than 90,000 periodicals worldwide. A keyword search feature allows online browsers to search the database for printed publications that report on all imaginable topics, from Arts and Crafts to Zebras. Freelance writers will find the MediaFinder helpful in locating publications worldwide that print articles in their specialty areas.

The Oxbridge system is designed for use by advertising and press personnel. Browsers receive catalog-style entries on print publications, both newspapers and magazines. The entries specify the target audience, publishing company, editor, frequency of issue, and advertising rates for each periodical. Freelance writers will find Oxbridge's online directories helpful in locating publications that purchase or print articles in their subject areas.

Newshare
http://www.newshare.com/

Newshare is an independent news and feature broker or syndicate. It is an interesting attempt to create a syndicate that handles the distribution and payment for journalistic works in an online environment. Authors or publishers can become contributing members. Members are slated to eventually gain royalties from a charge-per-page royalty system.

The Story Store
http://www.thestorystore.com

The Story Store is a clearinghouse that markets nonfiction articles to multiple markets. Authors may submit their nonfiction articles to the Story Store for resell to multiple markets. Writers receive 60 percent of the sales price while the Story Store retains 40 percent.

The Well
http://www.well.com/

The Well, originating from the San Francisco Bay Area, is one of the world's earliest online communities. Drop in on the Byline Conference to network with freelancers from around the world. A free trial visit can be made, and after that, subscriptions are $10 per month.

Working Writers
http://www.working-writers.com/

This New York City–based writers collective encourages freelance writers and translators in business, technical, journalistic, and Web areas to register with it for freelance assignments. The collective represents more than 100 registered writers and translators. Placements fees are charged to clients, not writers.

Writers@Work
http://www.together.net/~lifelong/writers.html

This site, put together by the authors of this book, archives freelance writing information and serves as a master directory to job banks and career resources online for writers. Some of the material in this chapter is extracted from our efforts to build this master online career site for professional writers. New career resources and writers' job banks will be continuously posted to this site.

The Electronic Classifieds—Newspaper Searches

If you have 175,000 job openings weekly, published in 30 newspapers across the United States, why not input them all into one giant online database that features a single keyword search system?

That's just what Internet technology allows, which is why online job search sites that glean material primarily from newspaper classifieds are springing up at amazing rates. Digitized newspaper databases, like CareerPath, allow job seekers to search for career openings nationwide—in some cases worldwide—from one convenient online site.

CareerPath
http://www.careerpath.com

CareerPath allows you to search through the classifieds of about 30 major metropolitan papers, among them the *Boston Globe*, the *Chicago Tribune*, the *Los Angeles Times*, *The New York Times*, the *San Jose Mercury News*, and *The Washington Post*. About 175,000 listings are archived here weekly. A companion Employers Profile section allows browsers to search for openings at selected large companies nationwide.

Editor & Publisher Interactive (EPI)
http://www.mediainfo.com/

Editor & Publisher maintains a database covering the online newspaper movement. If you're looking for a job in another region—even another continent—use the EPI newspaper database to locate the Web sites of small and regional newspapers. Then visit the Web sites of papers in areas that interest you to search their classifieds sections. Not all small papers put their classifieds section online, but the majority certainly do.

Super Job and Career Sites

Classified listings are ideally suited to database formatting, a popular computer function. And people always need jobs. It's no surprise, then, that what began as a minor industry experiment in the early 1990s, the online classified business, has become a booming enterprise.

Many of the largest super job sites on the Net, like E-Span, JobWeb, and the Monster Board, list tens of thousands of vacancies each week from companies nationwide. These sites can be employment gold mines, particularly if you work in a high-technology career writing niche such as interactive game scripting, technical and computer manual writing, or public relations and media marketing.

Many of the jobs listed for writers in these large databases are jobs for technical writers.

Business and industry writers may also find the super job sites helpful. Feature writers, reporters, humor writers, fiction or creative writers, and career freelancers will find little work listed at most super job sites, however. If you write for these beats, skip to the section on job sites specific to writers and literary types. These smaller, but more specialized, sites allow writers to zero in on the writing markets and on more freelance-related assignments as opposed to staff positions.

Searching a Super Job Site

Most super sites archive hundreds of thousands of employment opportunities weekly. As with all online databases, it pays to think about what you are searching for and experiment with search parameters at different sites if you want to pull up as many entries as possible that might apply to your career needs.

Keyword Searches

When executing keyword searches on large databases, try several key words. All databases do not classify jobs in the same manner. If you are looking for a writing job, try multiple keywords according to your specialty area: writer, journalist, reporter, magazine, editor, content developer, freelance, newspaper, media, and new media.

Categorical Searches

At some sites you begin your search by selecting a broad career category such as "media/publishing" or "marketing/public relations." CareerWeb is one super site that supports categorical searches. Study your menu of options before executing a categorical search. The categories provided by automated search systems do not always follow an intuitive logic. You may need to search across several categories to extract all the listings that suit your career needs.

Freelance Versus Staff Work

Most super site databases were not designed to separate out freelance from staff work. Databases that can accommodate such queries often require a keyword search on the word "contract" rather than the word "freelance." Experiment to see what works at varying sites.

Career Mosaic
http://www.service.com/cm/cm1.html

Mosaic's pages include a searchable database of more than 20 job newsgroups and a database of job openings worldwide that can be searched by geographic location or keyword. A free service called ResumeCM allows browsers to post resumes online.

CareerWeb
http://www.cweb.com/

CareerWeb lists primarily vacancies in technology and mainstream industry. Media and writing jobs can be gleaned from a search of categories in Publishing/ Media/Entertainment, Marketing/Communications/Sales, Public Relations/ Communications, and Technical Writing. A resume-posting service and career resource pointers are also provided.

E-SPAN Interactive Employment Network
http://www.espan.com

E-SPAN's job database allows searches by educational level, experience level, job level, salary requirements, geographic area, or keyword. Writing jobs are mainly technical or business related. The Career Companion section features links and listings for online education, travel and relocation resources, career assessment tools, indexes to research perspective companies, and professional networking hot spots. The ResumePro service allows browsers to submit resumes online or via e-mail.

FedWorld Information Network—Job Announcement Search
http://www.fedworld.gov

This master site supports an online search for career vacancies and job announcements within all branches of the federal government. Applicants can search for jobs by keyword or state location. The federal government hires writers, editors, public relations specialists, and a host of other media specialists.

JobWeb
http://www.jobweb.org

JobWeb is maintained by the National Association of Colleges and Employers. A special database allows college-aged surfers to locate internship or cooperative work placements. A search may also be completed on Federal Government Jobs. An Employer's Database allows searchers to pull up company profiles to learn about inhouse career and employment needs at leading corporations, such as Microsoft. Links are maintained to more than 50 online career resources.

Monster Board
http://monster.com

The Monster Board provides a searchable index of high-tech or computer-related jobs, mainly in the Northeast. Technical and business writers will want to visit this site often, but other writers will not find much of use here.

Online Career Center
http://www.occ.com/occ/

America's first Internet career center, the Online Career Center supports a keyword database for employment opportunities nationwide. Our keyword search on "writer" brought up more than 200 openings, mostly for technical, scientific, or documentation writers. Searches on words like "journalist" and "freelance" turned up ads also, including some top-notch career positions at national periodicals and newspapers.

TechJobs SuperSite
http://SuperSite.Net

TechJobs is a professional job bank and resource center where high-technology companies like Intel post career vacancies. Writers who specialize in technical documentation in engineering, computers, electronics, and the industry-training sectors will find limitless listings here.

Virtual Job Fair
http://www.vjf.com

The Virtual Job Fair is a magazine, a career fair, and a technical careers resource center. Outakes are offered from *High Technology Careers Magazine*, a resume-posting service is offered, and a job search database focusing on high-tech careers is maintained. Our keyword search for "writer" yielded 105 technology-related writing and editing jobs nationwide.

Job Sites for Writers and Literary Types

Academe This Week
http://chronicle.merit.edu

Academe This Week is the home page of academia's main newspaper, the weekly *Chronicle of Higher Education*. Colleges seeking faculty and administrators in English, creative writing, journalism, and other academic writing areas advertise here weekly.

Advertising Age—Monster Board Job Bank
http://www.adage.com/job_bank/index.html

Advertising Age, the printed industry publication, lists more than 700 jobs a week in advertising, media, and media-marketing areas.

Adweek's Classifieds
http://www.adweek.com/

Every Friday, *Adweek Magazine*, the print publication, posts its classifieds section to its Web site. Job listings include advertising, public relations, and media writing and management.

American Journalism Review's Newslink—JobLink Classifieds
http://www.newslink.org/

The *American Journalism Review* administers this super site for well-wired journalists. The JobLink section features career openings in traditional and new media. Staff positions and freelance opportunities in the United States and abroad are listed. Those seeking freelance work can also post their qualifications here. A Journalism Awards and Fellowship section details academic grants.

American Marketing Association—Jobs
http://www.ama.org/

The American Marketing Association, a leading association for marketing and public relations professionals, posts news and job announcements in marketing, research, and public relations to its Web site.

Arts Deadlines List
http://www.old.ircam.fr/divers/arts-deadlines.html

This is Richard Gardner's listing of scholarships, competitions, internships, and fellowships in the arts, including multimedia, creative writing, journalism, photography, and film.

Bricolage—Market Intelligence
http://bricolage.bel-epa.com/

Bricolage, an e-zine from the United Kingdom, sponsors a section called Market Intelligence. Editors in the United States and United Kingdom frequently post freelance-writing needs to the Market section

California Journalism Job Bank
http://www.csne.org/jobs/postings.htm/

This is the California Society of Newspaper Editors' ad board site for reporters, new media workers, and editors. Ads are primarily for West Coast newspapers and publishing enterprises.

CareerNet—Media Companies
http://www.careers.org/

CareerNet is a super site with more than 11,000 jobs posted each week, and more than 6,000 career-related resources and links. For listings specific to media, visit the Media Companies link in the Jobs Now section.

Comet.Net—Writer's Resources—Market News
http://www.comet.net/writersr/mktnews.htm

The Market News section of the Writer's Resource Center contains announcements of freelance job boards and online resource centers.

Copy Editor Job Board
http://www.copyeditor.com/scripts/jobfile.cgi

Career vacancies for copyeditors and proofreaders nationwide are posted to this fairly active resource board. Links and resource pointers of interest to editors are also provided.

Editor & Publisher Interactive
http://www.mediainfo.com/

Editor & Publisher, an industry newspaper, includes an interactive classifieds section. Classifieds include openings for newspaper professionals, cyberscribes, proofreaders, photo journalists, interns, and bureau chiefs. *Editor & Publisher* also maintains a database covering the online newspaper movement.

The Freelance Forum—Classifieds & Announcements
http://www.xs4all.nl/~scw/tff

This forum for freelance journalists and nonfiction writers features a classified jobs section for nonfiction authors and researchers.

Freelance Online
http://www.FreelanceOnline.com

Freelance Online posts jobs in writing, editing, instructional design, graphic arts, press production, and news syndication and press services. Freelancers can post notice of their availability for hire here also.

Inkspot—Classifieds & Markets
http://www.inkspot.com

This writers' resource page supports a Classifieds section where nonfiction freelance writers and editors can post their availability for hire, and a Market Information section that caters primarily to the fiction markets.

JAWS Job Bank—Journalism & Women's Symposium
http://www.jaws.org/jobs.html

JAWS is a nonprofit agency dedicated to promoting the advancement and well-being of women in the newsroom. Scholarship and journalism job opportunities are posted in the Job Bank section.

Journalism Jobs & Internships (J-Jobs)
http://www.journalism.berkeley.edu/resources/jobs/

This is a weekly digest of career opportunities culled from newsgroups, mailing lists, and other online resources. Listings are divided into four easy-to-search categories: journalism-related jobs, journalism internships, freelance opportunities, and journalism education positions.

National Diversity Journalism Job Bank
http://newsjobs.com

The Internet's largest free job-listing service for journalists posts career, freelance, and internship media vacancies nationwide. The site is maintained by journalism interns. The site also features a set of links to other media-related Job Banks online.

National Writers Union: Technical-Web-Multimedia Job Hotline
http://www.igc.apc.org/nwu/index.htm#Contents

The Hotline is a job-brokering project of the National Writers Union. Employers can list 1099-contract (freelance) positions online. Writers who locate jobs through the Hotline agree to pay a finder's fee of 10 percent of their first month's income.

NationJob Network—Advertising & Media Jobs Page
http://www.nationjob.com/media

NationJob maintains several job-page listings, one of which is especially for media professionals. Most jobs listed are staff positions with companies in the Midwest. Listings cover a range of writing careers from TV reporter to media buyer and public relations specialists.

Reporters Network—Jobs Board & Media Directory
http://www.reporters.net

This site for journalists is sponsored by Bob Sablatura, a reporter for the *Houston Chronicle*. Journalist and freelance job openings are posted on the Bulletin Board. Journalists are invited to post notices of their availability for work. Freelance journalists can also register their beat specialty in the master Media Directory.

SIMBA'S Job Forums
http://www.simbanet.com

Cowles/Simba, publisher of media newsletters and industry surveys, sponsors highly active Jobs Wanted and Jobs Offered message forums for media and new media writers, executives, programmers, and designers.

Society for Technical Communication—Employment
http://stc.org

The Society for Technical Communication (STC), the world's largest association for technical writers and communicators, posts job announcements and archives information on competitions and scholarships for technical communicators.

TV Jobs
http://www.tvjobs.com/

This site contains job listings from TV, broadcast, cable, and news bureaus nationwide. Listings include public relations, advertising, scripting, journalism, production positions, and intern openings. Resumes may also be submitted for employers to review.

Writers Guild of America—Interactive Writers Database
http://www.wga.org/

The Writers Guild of America (WGA) sponsors this database of authors for hire through the Guild who write in interactive—screen, script, video, and multimedia tutorial—realms for the entertainment, education and business markets.

The Writer's Marketboard
http://rain-crow-publishing.com/market/

The Marketboard is a forum for publishers to announce their needs for writing talent. Writers may also post announcements about works in progress for prospective publishers to review. Postings are accepted in literary, book, magazine, film, genre, technical, fiction, nonfiction, and journalistic markets. Writing contests, conferences, and scholarships are also posted here.

Ziff-Davis Net Job Database
http://www.zdnet.com/zdi/jobs/jobs.html

The computer book and magazine publisher Ziff-Davis sponsors this classified section, which accepts listings for high-technology positions, including technical writers, and multimedia and new media developers and marketers.

Fiction and Genre Markets

The Gila Queen's Guide to Markets
http://www.pacifier.com/~alecwest/gila/

The Gila Queen is a freelance market guide to publications and anthologies accepting fiction of varying types. Subscriptions cost $34 per year.

Inkspot—Writers' Classifieds: Markets
http://www.inkspot.com

This master writer's resource page supports a Market Information section that features primarily postings in non-paying fiction genre markets.

InterNovel Home Page
http://www.internovel.com/~novel

InterNovel is an experiment in which different authors are invited to submit chapters to an ongoing novel in romance or suspense, or a short story, or a work of poetry. The project aims to create coherent publishable works by merging the narrative streams of different authors and promises royalties to those who participate in publishable group writing experiments.

The Market List
http://www.greyware.com/marketlist/

Christopher Holliday maintains this one-stop short fiction resource center, which includes articles, interviews, and reviews, along with monthly listings of publishers' market needs in short fiction—sci-fi, horror, fantasy, and the speculative markets.

Mind's Eye Fiction
http://tale.com

Mind's Eye is an online clearinghouse that posts short story fiction to the World Wide Web. Browsers read the stories using a pay-per-view or micropayment system by opening up a credit charge account online. Rates vary, but online readers are generally charged from 18 to 66 cents for each story they read. Authors receive 75 percent royalty fees each time their story is viewed online by a new reader. Previously published stories are accepted.

Scavenger's Newsletter
http://users.aol.com/Lemarchand/scavenger.html

The "Scavenger's Newsletter" is a monthly surface mail newsletter for fiction writers working in horror, fantasy, and science fiction. Subscriptions are $17 per year.

The Scrivenery Marketplace
http://www.lit-arts.com/scriven.market.htm

The Scrivenery sponsors this site for fiction writers and poets. Scrivenery posts calls for manuscripts, announcements of literary contests and competitions, conference blurbs, writers' guidelines, and author-related promotional material to their Marketplace. Markets listed are small, literary, and primarily nonpaying.

Job-Related Newsgroups

The great news about Usenet newsgroups is that they can be used to locate jobs nationwide or worldwide in almost any industry. There are more than 50 job- and resume-posting newsgroups. Some are dedicated to specific professions (alt.journalism.freelance). Some are dedicated to regions (ne.jobs for New England jobs). Still others are dedicated to job postings in foreign countries (dk.jobs for jobs in Denmark).

For a master listing of job-related newsgroups, visit the Usenet Job Hunter's Companion <http://www.earthcon.com/jobs>. The Companion is a Web-based directory of job-related Usenet groups. Usenet groups for regional (e.g., Dallas/Ft. Worth) and international opportunities (e.g., Europe) are catalogued at this site.

This site is worth a visit to keep up to date on Usenet job groups or to determine if the geographic or international locations of interest to you support a special job newsgroup. The San Francisco Bay Area, for example, supports a special job newsgroup, ba.jobs.contract, that posts contract and freelance jobs in several areas. The Companion site is tied to a DejaNews search filter, so you can jump from here to search selected newsgroups from the DejaNews search site on the Web.

Newsgroup job boards are extremely active. The misc.jobs.offered newsgroup boasts a whopping 10,000 new postings every day or so. Misc.jobs.contract boasts a lot of traffic for contract or freelance opportunities for computer workers, programmers, and technical writers. The bad news is that, with this many job postings, how will you ever find what you need?

Unlike Web databases, Usenet newsgroups themselves have no inherent search capability. They operate like huge public bulletin boards with people tacking up new announcements every second of the day. You have to literally flip through all the announcements every day or two to see what's listed.

You could spend hours scrawling through tens of thousands of message postings in an effort to ferret out the ones that might apply to you. Luckily, some of the super job and career sites on the Web now support special search engines that have been creatively harnessed to job newsgroups to make them searchable by keyword. We recommend the use of the following special Web sites to bring a keyword search logic to your job search efforts through newsgroups.

Career Magazine
http://www.careermag.com/

The Career Magazine, a super site, downloads and indexes job announcements from all job-related newsgroups every day. Use their search engine to sort and sift by keyword for postings that might suit you from all the job-related newsgroups. We searched under "writer" and received 135 job postings, almost all for technical or product-documentation writers. Our search on "journalists" pulled up 16 entries, mostly in corporate public relations.

Career Mosaic—jobs.offered
http://www.service.com/cm/cm1.html

Mosaic's pages allow for a clean and quick full-text search of more than 20 job and resume-related newsgroups by keyword.

Newsletter Classifieds

@Writers

The Market section of this electronic newsletter features paying and non-paying markets. To subscribe, send e-mail to <majordomo@samurai.com> with "subscribe a-writers" in the body of the e-mail. Back issues may be retrieved from <http://www.geocities.com/Athens/Acropolis/6608/>.

Inklings: Newsletter for Writers on the Net

The Market section of this bimonthly newsletter features freelance pay and no-pay opportunities. If you have a book coming out, you can send a blurb to "Inklings" for promotional inclusion in their Subscriber section. To subscribe, send e-mail to <majordomo@samurai.com> with "subscribe inklings" in the body of the e-mail. Information and back issues may also be accessed via the Web at <http://www.inkspot.com/inklings>.

Media Professional

The Help Wanted section of Media Professional features career openings in news and media writing, sales, marketing, and distribution. Back issues of Media Professional are accessible on the Web, <http://www.accessabc.com>. To subscribe, send e-mail to MediaProfl@aol.com. In the body of the message type <subscribe your name>.

Writers Page

The Market and Resources section of this weekly newsletter contains freelance writing information. Columnists respond to real-life dilemmas and questions on the writing life. To subscribe, e-mail WritersPage-request@niestu.com, with the single word <subscribe> in the subject line. Back issues are archived at <http://www.getset.com/writers/>.

CHAPTER 4

Browsing the Electronic Newsstand: *Magazines, Newspapers, and Journals*

New media—that's what it's called when media bypasses paper, ink, and delivery trucks, arriving at the computer stations of the masses in bits and bytes. New media has literally come unbound. As this book goes to press, everyone is trying to figure out what new media is and how to turn its production into an income-generating (rather than cash-sucking) enterprise.

Whether printed or digitized, the message appears to stay the same. It's the delivery mechanisms that are changing—rapidly. The Gutenberg press wrested information from the archives of the elite, casting it like printed pearls toward the masses. The Internet is making every child with a modem a Johannes Gutenberg all over again.

What does it mean that any child can create his or her own newspaper and fling it electronically around the world and back again for only pennies? What should a virtual newspaper look like? Is there a market for women's magazines on the World Wide Web? Who's going to pay to keep online media afloat? Subscribers? Advertisers?

No one has the answers to these and other questions yet, but lively discussions are afoot. *Editor & Publisher Interactive* <http://www.mediainfo.com/> is a must read for newspaper journalists and industry experts wanting to gauge the directive flow of digital ink. The Web edition of this print-based newspaper posts features, hosts interesting columns on trends in cybermedia, and houses an open archive.

For an annual report on what journalists themselves think, click in at MediaSource <http://www.mediasource.com>. The text of *Media in Cyberspace: The Nation's Largest Study of Journalists' Use of Cyberspace* is housed here. This survey of more than 600 newspaper and magazine editors, conducted by Middleburg & Associates and the Columbia University Graduate School of Journalism, is slated to be an annual event.

MediaCentral <http://www.mediacentral.com>, from Cowles New Media, is a hot spot for news on cybermedia drifts and directions. This site houses an annual report and a discussion forum on the "Role of Magazines in the New Media Age" through a partnership with Northwestern University's Medill School of Journalism. Read the report to gain a glimpse into what industry pioneers like Ziff-Davis, Newsweek, and Hearst think of new media.

If you're a newspaper editor or publisher who feels perplexed about the purpose of an online edition, then the "1996 New Media Project" report published by the American Society of Newspaper Editors (ASNE) <http://www.asne.org> is a must read. This definitive report, archived online, looks at the answers to scores of crucial industry questions like "Why should I bother with all this new media stuff," and "Can I do this on the cheap?"

If you want to participate in the intellectual melee at the electronic frontier personally, sign up for the discussion lists maintained by Steve Outing of the *Planetary News*. Outing may be familiar to some from his new media column in *Editor & Publisher Interactive*. The Online-News list allows journalists and news executives to discuss the uncertain evolution of newspapers and magazines from print to electronic form. To subscribe, send e-mail to <majordomo@planetarynews.com> with the message "subscribe online-news" in the body of your e-mail.

A related list, Online-Newspapers, is restricted to newspaper researchers and professionals involved in the interactive news industry. For subscription information, e-mail Steve Outing <steve@planetarynews.com> with a personal note about your professional affiliations.

In this chapter, we highlight what's happening in the world of electronic news media. We give you the success stories, as well as commentary on enterprises that may have come unplugged by the time you crack the spine on this old media opus.

While we include an annotated directory of recommended sites to visit, our directories are by no means exhaustive. They are simply illustrative of the best in news, journalism, and innovative online design as we go to press.

Magazines: Online Trends

Anyone who could illuminate the human need that a magazine fulfills might also be able to prognosticate what people should crave in the way of an online edition. But magazines are odd media creatures. They are not chock full of terse information that changes daily—as are newspapers. Magazines are sexier than newspapers. Prone to more pictures, more opinion, more features that cut beyond the newsy facts to the meat of the matter at hand. Magazines are more relaxed than the news. Slicker, prettier, easier to read—yet still amazingly informative.

What Does an Electronic Magazine Look Like?

In an article for *New Media Week* we explored what was happening to magazines as they jump from the printed page onto the cathode tube. We stand by our conclusion in that review: These are not your mother's magazines. Electronic magazines differ from their print counterparts in two key ways: They are generally interactive rather than static, inviting readers to participate in the articles and other content once they are online; and they commonly act as resource centers by sponsoring online forums or chats that enrich or extend the coverage given to selected topics on the printed page.

Most electronic editions play on the concept that readers crave interactive gathering places and resource centers. *Home Office Computing* and *Small Business Computing*, Scholastic SOHO Group magazines whose readership is by definition well wired, host an impressive electronic media presence. *Home Office* archives its print edition back to January 1995, on America Online's Newsstand. While the article archive may be the core of what *Home Office* has to offer, it is far from the end-all and be-all of *Home Office* online.

On America Online, *Home Office* supports weekly live chats with the editors, free business forums with experts on everything from taxes to international marketing, and message boards where readers can connect with each other to discuss home-based business matters.

The "Home Office/Small Business" Web site is yet another creature. Termed *Your Small Office*, the site extends its expertise to the gathering of links to great online business sites, providing interactive self-tests on small-business matters and posting fun business horoscopes. An impressive library of free downloadable business demo software and computer-ready templates is also maintained online.

Time-Warner's Pathfinder and Ziff-Davis's ZD Net are two examples of media giants building online resource centers that transcend their print publications. Both sites allow browsers to access samples and archives from numerous flagship print publications; both sites also offer extended interactive features like Ziff-Davis's LearnItOnline, a subscription-based online tutorial service for learning new business software applications.

New Media Magazine Enterprises

In addition to forcing printed magazines to regroup as interactive enterprises, the Net has encouraged the development of completely new media ventures. One of the most interesting trends has been the rise of cultural/literary magazines; *Word*, *Feed*, *Salon*, and *Slate* are a few of the front-runners.

Microsoft's *Slate*, a cultural magazine, was launched on the World Wide Web in June 1996, amid much fanfare and an equal amount of skepticism. *Slate* threw the new media scene into a frenzy when it announced that, rather than remaining free as are most online editions, it would behave as a true magazine and would charge online readers a subscription fee. *Slate* later backed down from charging subscription fees, except to those who prefer to receive the magazine in its print form. It remains advertisement driven, running at a loss.

Magazines are emerging in bolder electronic forms than are daily newspapers. They also appear to be failing or scaling back their electronic forms at a higher rate than other media. The *Utne Reader*, the Minneapolis-based *Reader's Digest* for progressives, launched an ambitious Web site in 1994. The site supported features not found in the monthly print edition, and it went even further by creating online "literary salons" for the discussion of these features as well as themes from the print edition. *Utne* had barely opened its electronic doors, however, when costs outpaced revenue (as with most magazines, whether online or in print, the site was budgeted to run on advertising revenue), causing the enterprise to stop producing original content. The current scaled-back version, termed *The Utne Cafe*, consists primarily of a conferencing site where the literate digerati gather to butt ideological heads.

Rather then charge subscriptions to individuals, most electronic editions today are betting on advertising dollars and strategic partnerships with high-traffic commercial gateways like America Online to sustain them in the long run. Most are taking losses on immediate electronic endeavors in the belief that if they build it, readers and advertisers will someday come. This is by no means a sure strategy. As this book goes to press, some magazines are pulling down their Web sites, while still others are racing to release electronic editions.

Directory of Magazines

The Atlantic Monthly—Atlantic Unbound
http://www2.theAtlantic.com/atlantic/

In 1993, the oldest continuously printed magazine in America, the *Atlantic Monthly* (founded in 1857), went online as a flagship publication on America Online's Newsstand. *Atlantic Unbound* today archives content, offers online-only features, links current articles to "flashback" historical pieces on the same topics, and proffers downloadable audio of printed poetry. Post & Riposte is a chat forum where readers exchange opinions on cultural currents.

Epicurious
http://www.epicurious.com/a_home/a00_home/home.html

Epicurious, a CondeNet publication, is an online feast of features for gourmets. The site includes book reviews, restaurant guides, and recipes. Main sections include Eating, Drinking, and Playing with Your Food. Discussion forums (such as All You Do Is Wine) allow readers to swap tips about the good gustatory life.

Feed
http://www.feedmag.com

Feed is a new Web-based magazine that spins left-of-center cultural and political commentary. Articles cover issues and trends in the arts, politics, music, media, and the online life. Discussion forums, called Dialogs, encourage readers to rant and rave about featured topics.

Home Office Computing and Small Business Computing
http://www.smalloffice.com

The sister print magazines *Home Office Computing* and *Small Business Computing*, both from the Scholastic SOHO publishing group, host the Your Small Office Web site; this features links to online business resources, a free business software library, and expert advice forums.

Internet World
http://www.iw.com

Internet World is a top-circulating magazine on Internet issues. It is rich in the coverage of Net business trends and technology. Back issues, online tips, and resource links are archived online.

Poets & Writers
http://www.pw.org

Poets & Writers is a national print literary magazine that publishes interviews, essays, and information on conferences, grants, and business matters for poets and fiction writers. Summaries of current and back issues are archived online. The magazine sponsors an online Speakeasy where writers and poets can engage each other in dialogue on the literary life.

Salon
http://www.salonmagazine.com

In 1995, in the middle of a San Francisco newspaper strike, *Salon* was conceived as a West Coast online literary and cultural magazine. Replenished daily in its online version, *Salon* is a "two-thumbs up" literary success. Books, literature, dining, culture, and the writing life are pursued with more gusto than in any other magazine—digital or otherwise. Novelist Anne Lamott pens "Word by Word," a public diary on the writing life. The interactive Table Talk forum invites readers to have their intellectual say in issues as covered or uncovered by *Salon*.

Slate
http://www.slate.com/

The magazine *Slate*, sponsored by Microsoft, features first-rate political and social commentary as well as The Fray, a readers' comment and debate board that reports an impressive 20,000 visits or "hits" per week. Content from *Slate* is sometimes repurposed or reprinted in *Time* and other print publications.

Time-Warner—Pathfinder
http://www.pathfinder.com

This super site from multimedia giant Time-Warner bundles magazine samples and back issue archives, companion chats, debate boards, mailing lists, and a subscription-based personal news delivery service. It previews and searches *Time*, *Life*, *The Netly News*, *Money*, *People*, *Fortune*, and other flagship publications. News, games, and information on how to navigate the Net make this site a must see for online newbies and new media idealists.

Utne Reader
http://www.utne.com/

The Minneapolis-based eclectic reader posts the best of the alternative press to its Web site each month. Visitors can read articles from the print edition, enter the online Cafe to chat with like-minded souls about invigorating social issues, or register to receive via e-mail the Utne-Buzz—announcements about the *Reader* and its online events.

Wired—HotWired
http://www.wired.com

Wired, issued from the technologically hot-and-hip San Francisco Bay Area, came from out of nowhere to become the cultural voice of the "wired" generation. *Wired*, the print magazine, covers the digital revolution across media networks and delivery systems: cable, TV, Internet, and satellite. There is an online archive as well as a host of Wired enterprises and spin-offs, including a search engine (HotBot) and late-breaking news.

Word
http://www.word.com

Some argue that the multimedia ability of the Net will change what a story is about dramatically and forever. Tom Lavaccari and Dan Pelson, and their dramatists, essayists, and journalists at *Word*, an innovative online writing enterprise (of sorts), agree with this premise. They publish features online that have to do with "issues, culture, saliva." The Talk Inn, a chat forum, encourages yakkety-yak back from online browsers.

Ziff-Davis—ZD Net
http://www.zdnet.com

Ziff-Davis sponsors this super online computing resource center with news blurbs, features, downloadable software samples and games, and archive access from flagship Ziff-Davis print publications like *PC Magazine*, *PC Week*, *Computer Life*, *MacUser*, *Computer Gaming*, and *Internet User*.

Finding Magazines Online

American Journalism Review—Newslink
http://www.newslink.org/mag.html

The *American Journalism Review's* magazine index is exceptionally well designed, allowing browsers to sort and search by type of magazine, country of origin (United States or Canada), or specific magazine title.

Ecola Directories: Newsstand
http://www.ecola.com

Ecola's online newsstand offers a blue-ribbon set of links to online magazine editions. The magazine links are organized by subject area, such as health or business, and country of origin. A search feature allows browsers to input the name of a specific magazine.

The Electronic Newsstand
http://www.enews.com/

The Electronic Newsstand features the Monster Magazine List, a search engine that locates online magazines by name or topic area. It also allows for a limited search of the archives of online magazines. While few magazines digitize their complete editions, many print magazines, like *The New Yorker*, can be sampled online from this site.

Newspapers: Online Trends

It's no secret that newspapers have hit hard times. Declining circulation since the early 1990s has resulted in dropping advertising dollars, while escalating production costs have mercilessly pinched at slim profit margins. When the

United States headed online in hoards, news producers hoped that newspapers might be digitized in a way that would increase their circulation numbers, thereby increasing their advertising revenue, while simultaneously cutting production costs by virtually eliminating the need for paper, ink, and delivery personnel. The daily news online: It was an idea whose time had come.

The *San Jose Mercury News*, published in the heart of California's Silicon Valley technological quake zone, was the first printed paper to go online, in a 1993 partnership with the commercial service America Online (AOL). The *Mercury News* is still online, though it has left AOL and now operates independently on the World Wide Web where it maintains a rich array of pay-per-view news from the archives of twenty-four Gannett newspapers nationwide.

What Does a Digital Newspaper Look Like?

There are no hard rules about what an online newspaper must look like, nor how such ventures will economically sustain themselves. As with all media, advertising remains the favored source of support. But pay-per-view schemes, where online users open accounts and are charged small fees for each article downloaded in full-text version, are gaining support with Web-based editions.

Many papers look online as they do in print. *USA Today*, the electronic edition, for example, is an immediately recognizable synoptic twin to the printed *USA Today*; one difference is that when you read the daily news from your computer screen you won't walk away with ink on your fingers.

Most newspapers do not post their full print editions online. *The Wall Street Journal Interactive* does offer full-text retrieval, but it also charges an annual subscription fee for this enhanced sort of "home delivery" or search ability via the World Wide Web.

Charging a subscription fee to access a Web-based electronic edition was—and remains—a bold move. It appears to have worked for *The Wall Street Journal Interactive*, a paper known for its timely delivery of news on vital financial trends. In February 1997, the *Journal* announced that with 70,000 paid online subscribers it was the number-one subscriber-supported business news source on the Web. Subscribers to *The Wall Street Journal Interactive* get more than the street edition of the *Journal;* they also get an electronic feed into 3,600 business news services.

Directory of Online Newspapers

American Reporter
http://www.american-reporter.com

America's first daily, independent, digital newspaper, edited by Joe Shea of Hollywood, California, is cooperatively owned by the far-flung correspondents who produce it.

Boston Globe
http://www.boston.com/globe/glohome.htm

The *Boston Globe* posts news and feature works, offering cybercruisers a rich electronic gateway into the cultural, political, and entertainment duchy of Boston. Online discussion forums encourage readers to plunk down their opinions on news and cultural events before moving on. The Living/Arts forum draws commentary from writers and artists. An electronic search can draw from the last fifteen years of staff-written material, but only full-text material from the "today" or "yesterday" issue can be retrieved for free. Back issue material is sold through a pay-per-view online account system.

Chicago Sun-Times
http://www.suntimes.com/

This site contains headline news, sports, business, columns, and the classifieds from the windy city's favorite daily news feed, the *Chicago Sun-Times*. Travelers headed to Chicago will want to check out the rich entertainment, restaurant, and regional calendar of events online before arriving in the cultural metropolis of the Midwest. News junkies will be disappointed to find no archive of full feature articles, however.

Christian Science Monitor
http://www.csmonitor.com

The electronic edition of the *Monitor* is a meaty, free read of top national and international news. A search feature pulls articles and editorials from an easy-to-use archive that chronicles the nation's past in rich, full-text detail. The Forum encourages interactive feedback on the news. The Our Place Books section archives book reviews, houses a set of Best Books links, and supports an interactive Book-Chat Forum. Browsers can subscribe to the *Monitor* and receive a personalized e-mail edition for $15 per quarter—costs subject to change.

Financial Times—FT.com
http://www.usa.ft.com

Access headline international news in business, economics, and finance as gleaned from London's esteemed *Financial Times*, an international, English-language, daily business paper in print since 1888. Access to abbreviated daily issues and an online archive is free to those who register to obtain the paper via the World Wide Web. A peek into the Business Books section or a keyword search on "books" turns up interesting news on business books and the publishing industry in the United Kingdom. The *Times*'s quarterly "Business Books Review" is accessible online.

The Los Angeles Times
http://www.latimes.com/HOME/

Summaries of national and regional stories are posted to the Web daily. The *Los Angeles Times* gets top marks for ease of navigation and delightful page-like designs. If you're relocating to Los Angeles, JobSource and HomeSource render employment ads and home rental opportunities keyboard clickable. The site also supports a directory of regional resources (including a nude beach guide) and entertainment news. There is an archive search service, but it's fee based, with prices set at varying rates for searches and full-text retrieval either online or by FAX from the *Times*'s research department.

The New York Times
http://www.nytimes.com/

Read feature articles and news summaries daily online. Late-breaking news is posted after 1 P.M. each day. Bibliophiles will be delighted to find that the Book Review section boasts a free Herculean archive of 50,000 reviews, dating back to 1980. The first chapters of recently reviewed books are accessible online. Take a seat at the Round Table or Book Biz forums to discuss publishing with other online literates. The CyberTimes section and archive is a great read for those interested in online trends.

The San Jose Mercury News
http://www.sjmercury.com

America's first printed newspaper to enter cyberspace (in 1993), the *Mercury News*, a Knight-Ridder newspaper, now hosts its own Web site, Mercury Center, offering news and culture online from the Silicon Valley of California as well as a great free news-fetch and desktop-delivery service, NewsHound. Browsers can search the archives of the *Mercury News* and other Knight-Ridder papers online, accessing over 1 million articles printed since the mid-1980s. Headline and first paragraph peeks are free, but browsers who desire full-text retrieval are required to pay by the piece.

USA Today
http://www.usatoday.com/

USA Today, a Gannett newspaper, pops up on the computer screen with the same recognizable look as the streetside edition. News, weather, sports, money, and life are awarded blurb-like coverage in the daily electronic edition.

Village Voice
http://www.villagevoice.com

The Big Apple's best known alternative cultural weekly is as electrifying online as it is in print. The online entertainment, personals, and job listings are must reads for anyone who is New York City bound. The "Voice Literary Supplement" is a clickable delight for literature and book lovers. Chat salons operate for those who crave live minds to bounce around with when online.

The Wall Street Journal Interactive
http://wsj.com

Promotional features and excerpts from "Today's Edition" of *The Wall Street Journal* are posted online. The Small Business Suite, an area of news and resources for home-based businesses and entrepreneurs, is also sample-ready at the site.

The WashingtonPost.com
http://www.washingtonPost.com/

Read the current day's *Washington Post* online or search the last fourteen days of the paper by keyword topic of interest. The Chapter One section allows browsers to make a free perusal of the first chapter of books reviewed in the *Post*. The Talk section encourages opinionated readers to talk back to editors about hot issues and controversial news coverage.

Finding Newspapers Online

American Journalism Review (AJR)—Newslink
http://www.newslink.org/

The *American Journalism Review*'s Newslink is the stellar newspaper index on the Internet. The site includes links and contact information on U.S., foreign, and campus papers. Links are organized according to helpful categories: major metros, national newspapers, by state, daily, weekly, alternative, business, special markets, as well as levels of service. The *AJR* also posts some of the best digitally enhanced news about online media trends.

Arastar Internet News Page
http://www.arastar.net/news/

This all-in-one index categorizes newspaper links in the United States by type of news, national and regional coverage, and the paper's state of origin. International newspaper links run the gamut from the *Turkish Times* to the *Katmandu Post* of Nepal. The index favors newspapers but includes a mix of other prominent media also.

Association of Alternative Newsweeklies
http://aan.eline.com/

The Association represents more than 100 nondaily, primarily free circulation, alternative newspapers in North America. News, events, and membership activities as well as a comprehensive directory of alternative member papers are housed online.

Ecola Directories—Newsstand
http://www.ecola.com

Ecola's online newsstand offers a blue-ribbon set of links to online newspapers. The newspaper links are organized by country of origin, from Africa to South America. A search feature allows browsers to input the name of specific newspapers. The United States Newspapers sub-index sorts newspapers by two types, business or alternative, then by region of operation.

Editor & Publisher—Database Directory of the World's Online Newspapers
http://www.mediainfo.com/

Editor & Publisher, a news industry publication, supports this directory to more than 1,700 newspapers worldwide. Browsers can search by country of origin, state of origin, or the title of the publication.

Media Encyclopedia
http://www.geocities.com/CollegePark/4331/

The Media Encyclopedia is a specialized index to university and professional newspapers, developed and maintained by Louis Gray, online manager for the *Daily Californian* at the University of California Berkeley.

Newspaper Mania
http://www.club.innet.be/~year0230/american.htm

Mania is an ambitious hot link system to more than 1,400 online newspapers worldwide. Mania includes listings for North America, South America, Africa, Asia, Europe, and the Middle East.

Journals and E-Zines: Online Trends

Digital journals take varying forms. Content-heavy scientific and educational journals tend to take text-based forms for easy reading and downloading. When viewing a specialty journal online, all you may get is text. The message is the meat.

Literary and cultural journals tend to take more experimental forms. In the e-zine world, or the world of small, independent magazines, both content and format may be nontraditional. Many e-zines exist only in electronic form, either on the Web in hyperlink form or via e-mail in digest form. With e-zines and experimental journals, the medium may become a part of the message.

What Does a Digital Journal Look Like?

The Paris Review has been around for five decades in its print form, so experimentation remains mild in its electronic form. There is one notable electronic facelift to the *Review* online: downloadable audio clips allow browsers to listen to Woody Allen, for example, as he reads his own words aloud.

The *Columbia Journalism Review* has been rolling off the presses since 1961. Online, it persists in tackling the difficult issues that journalists face, but it also extends itself to the task of providing electronic history lessons as told in interview form by those who lived through journalism's decisive moments this century. The War Stories section lets browsers read through interview texts with leading journalists (like Ben Bagdikian of *The Washington Post*) while playing audio and visual clips in a separate but joined scroll frame. The result is an engaging multimedia view into history, like peering through an early kinescope.

Directory of Online Journals

Columbia Journalism Review
http://www.cjr.org/

The *Columbia Journalism Review*, put out bimonthly by the Columbia School of Journalism at Columbia University, is the oldest media-monitoring publication in the United States. Articles, essays, and opinions tackle the difficult issues facing journalists today, from ethics to the effects of technology. Back issues are archived online.

George Jr.
http://www.georgejr.com

George Jr. is a "literary lark-about for readers with brains." There really is a George Jr.: George Myers, Jr., books editor for the *Columbus Dispatch* in Ohio. Some of America's best contemporary writers are digitized by *George Jr.* in fictive, essay, review, journalistic, and poetic form. Music, art, film, books, and current events are chronicled in each issue.

Grand Street
http://www.grand-street.com/

Grand Street is a renowned quarterly cultural and literary magazine that tackles sticky theme topics (for example, the fetishes issue) and publishes emerging ideologists, artists, and authors in fictive, journalistic, poetic, and essay form. The current printed issue is posted online. Back issues are archived under a "flashbacks" rubric.

Mississippi Review Web
http://sushi.st.usm.edu/mrw

The *Mississippi Review* is a national literary journal of new and established voices published twice yearly by the University of Southern Mississippi's Center for Writers graduate school program. The Web edition is issued monthly and features a back issues archive. Information is provided on submissions and the creative writing program itself.

The Paris Review
http://www.voyagerco.com/PR/

The *Review* is an internationally acclaimed print-based literary journal, edited by George Plimpton. Excerpts from the quarterly publication are online, along with an archive of cutting-edge poetry, fiction, and literary features. Audio downloads give the *Review* a slight multimedia twang.

Yellow Silk
http://www.enews.com/magazines/yellow_silk/

Yellow Silk is a print-based, high-brow journal of the erotic arts. The journal features stories, photographs, and art prints of tasteful, culturally inspired erotica for modern readers regardless of their sex or sexual orientation. Excerpts from current and back issues are archived online.

Finding Journals Online

Association of Research Libraries Directory of Electronic Journals & Newsletters
http://arl.cni.org/scomm/edir

The Association has published a print directory to e-journals since 1991. The sixth edition is online. This is a super online reference to academic, professional, mainstream, and literary periodicals. The online directory includes links to Web sites as well as e-mail links to editorial contacts at each publication.

The Electronic Newsstand
http://www.enews.com/

The Electronic Newsstand features the Monster Magazine List, a search engine that locates mainstream journals by name or topic area. Many print journals, like *Yellow Silk*, can be sampled and subscribed to online from this site.

E-Zines: The Ultimate Magazine Database
http://www.dominis.com/Zines/

E-Zines is a grade-A search system for locating journals, magazines, and online literary chapbooks. The index can be searched by category (Fiction & Poetry or Humor, for example) or by title of the publication. Scientific journals are less well represented, while alternative Net-based small enterprises (that is, e-zines) are previewed more heavily.

John Labovitz's E-Zine List
http://www.meer.net/~john/e-zine-list/index.html

A master worldwide directory of electronically distributed 'zines or small magazines available on the Internet or through e-mail. E-zines are small, nonprofit, and generally nonpaying enterprises that typically cover subculture or niche market concerns. Many are experimental or offbeat. Some simply have small circulations.

NewJour Electronic Journals & Newsletters Archive
http://gort.ucsd.edu/newjour

Maintained by University of California San Diego librarian James Jacob, the archive for the NewJour Internet mailing list is an awesome achievement that links to 3,500 electronic journals or e-journals, some of them funky and literary, while many are professional or academic on specialized topics from Christian music to the science of experimental algorithms. The one downside is that searches can be done only alphabetically by title, not by subject area.

Xines Online Newsstand
http://www.kumo.swcp.com/xines

Xines, a project of Desert Moon Periodicals of New Mexico, is an international distributor for alternative and small-press publications. Content and subscription information is provided on more than 1,000 alternative magazines such as *Temp Slave* and *babysue*. Browsers can order online. Entries can be viewed by subject category (from piercing to poetry to gay girlfriends) or by alphabetical order.

Researching Online:
Reference Works and News Search Services

The Internet is the world's largest library and public records hall. Its digitized stacks literally never end. Information abounds. Using free online databases and directories, we've successfully located everything from the phone numbers of lost loves, to statistical background data on seniors who cybercruise, to the number of canines born in captivity in 1990. This chapter catalogs the best cybersleuth sites for researching online.

If you research regularly for selected markets, read the last section of this chapter—on electronic newsrooms and news clipping and search services—carefully. That section details free and fee-based news clipping services that will, on command, deliver specialized news to your desktop daily. It also details the best databases and resource centers for searching for background material online.

Finding People

You've just read the comments of an expert in an article and have decided that you want to interview that person for an article on a related theme. You wonder, could you connect with that person, who lives in Saudi Arabia, via e-mail?

Ironically, locating people online is sometimes easier than locating them in the real world, though the process is much the same. The Internet houses a bonanza of free directories designed for locating people and businesses—phone numbers, street addresses, and e-mail addresses—worldwide.

AT&T 800 Directory
http://www.tollfree.att.net/dir800

Forget dial-in directory assistance and the charges associated with using it. Search for AT&T toll-free 800 numbers online.

Four11—The Internet White Pages
http://www.four11.com

This is a searchable directory of 7 million e-mail addresses for the whole Internet. If you want to make it easy for others to find you, register your e-mail address here for free. If you're searching for the e-mail address of your favorite author, or a long-lost beau, this is a great first-search spot.

InfoSpace
http://www.infospace.com

This is a super set of directories to residential, business, and toll-free phone numbers, street addresses, and e-mail addresses, and companion business and government Web sites in the United States and Canada.

Switchboard
http://www.switchboard.com/

Switchboard boasts a Find People and Find Business directory of more than 106 million residential entries and 11 million business listings. Name searches yield geographical addresses and telephone numbers culled from public directory listings nationwide. This is the most comprehensive online phone and surface mail directory.

WhoWhere?
http://www.whowhere.com/

This is a searchable directory of e-mail addresses, phone numbers, surface addresses, personal home pages, government home pages, and Internet phone numbers for people, businesses, and organizations.

Finding Experts

Need to locate an expert to interview for that piece you've been assigned on toxic waste conversion systems? The Net can help you locate experts quickly and efficiently. Online systems like Ask the Expert make finding an expert as easy as dialing up a Web site.

If you've authored a book, quite a few newspeople would probably love to use you as a background expert for their own research and work. In turn, getting quoted or referenced in news, magazine, and trade publications will help you to build your reputation and sell your books and services.

If you write frequently in a specialized area, visit the following sites to register yourself as an expert who is willing to provide background fodder for reporters on the prowl.

Ask the Expert
http://wwwpitsco.com/p/askexperts.html

This Web site offers more than 200 links and e-mail addresses for online experts.

The Expertise Center
http://www.expertcenter.com/

This is a database of experts that includes brief online biographies and contact information.

GuestFinder
http://www.GuestFinder.com

This is Lorilyn Bailey's Web-based directory of authors, experts, and spokespeople available to speak to the media.

ProfNet
http://www.vyne.com/profnet

The State University of New York at Stony Brook administers this online database for journalists looking for experts to interview. More than 2,000 public relations officers from more than 800 universities, government branches, and industries in the United States and abroad are available for expert commentary. Send an e-mail query to <profnet@vyne.com> outlining your needs. Or visit the Web site where you can access an online database.

Online Experts
http://www.experts.com/

A searchable database of experts accessible online.

Finding Government Resources

When searching for national, regional, or statewide statistical information—from the population of Nebraska to the nearest federal park with camping facilities—the Internet is a gold mine of governmental tidbits. We list the following super sites for inaugurating a governmental search.

The Federal Web Locator
http://www.law.vill.edu/Fed-Agency/fedwebloc.html

The Villanova Center for Information Law and Policy maintains this laudable index to sites maintained by the federal government on the Web. A search engine allows for sweep searches on key terms.

FedWorld Information Network
http://www.fedworld.gov/

FedWorld is an electronic gateway to more than 150 federal government agencies. This site collects government gophers, file transfer protocol (FTP) sites, and Web pages into a clearly categorized, easy-to-search system.

Infomine
http://lib-www.ucr.edu/govpub/

The University of California sponsors this site that makes locating state and federal government information online a snap. Keyword, document title, and subject searches are accommodated.

United States Federal Government Agencies Page
http://www.lib.lsu.edu/gov/fedgov.html

The U.S. Federal Government Agencies Page of Louisiana State University's Library Division is an impressive list of links to government Internet gateways, including gophers and Web pages. Executive, judicial, legislative, independent, quasi-governmental, and boards' and commissions' links are provided.

Directory of Key Government Sites

Congress.Org
http://congress.org/

This is a complete directory and informational archive on members of the U.S. Congress and Senate. The site also includes information on House and Senate subcommittees.

Supreme Court: Decisions Database
http://www.law.cornell.edu/supct/

Cornell University's Legal Information Institute maintains this online archive of U.S. Supreme Court decisions made since 1990.

THOMAS: Legislative Information on the Internet
http://www.thomas.loc.gov/

THOMAS is a searchable database of the legislative activities and proceedings of the U.S. Congress. THOMAS is a project of the Library of Congress.

The White House
http://www.whitehouse.gov/

Visit here for a virtual tour of the White House and its gardens. Welcome sound bytes are archived here from the president and vice president. Historical facts and background information on the Executive Branch are given.

Library Resources

Libraries are home to writers of all stripes. Now you can electronically access the professional staff, research services, and special collections of the Library of Congress, as well as dial up the card catalogs and reference desks of thousands of libraries worldwide.

If you research from home, check with your local and state library systems about dial-in searches on card catalog holdings and any special text or document retrieval services that may be available to you locally via your modem.

If you're searching for key resource sites online in any subject, stop by the evolving Internet Reference Desks maintained by the WWW Virtual Library Project or Argus Associates. These guides to subject-specific hot spots on the Web will point you in the right direction.

Libraries Online

Library of Congress
http://www.loc.gov/

Retrieve public documents and computer search the card catalog, special collections, and databases of the nation's largest public library directly from the World Wide Web. The Library of Congress is also set up to allow access and search of the card catalogs and holdings of hundreds of other libraries nationwide, both university and government-supported institutions.

University of California Berkeley Digital Library—Libraries on the Web—Libweb
http://sunsite.berkeley.edu/LibWeb

This is an awesome directory of electronic gateways into public, academic, and specialized libraries and archives in the United States, Canada, and designated foreign countries. Jump off here into the lobbies of more than 1,000 libraries, from the National Sporting Library of Middleburg, Virginia, to the Black Film Archive at Indiana University.

Dictionaries Online

Anita Nuopponen's Online Dictionaries & Glossaries
http://www.uwasa.fi/comm/termino/collect

Anita Nuopponen of the University of Vassa, Finland, maintains this four-star worldwide dual directory of foreign language and special terminology dictionaries that are housed online. Language dictionaries range from Afrikaans to Urdu. The Term-Online directory indexes dictionaries in terminology areas from Agriculture to Vehicles.

Dictionaries
http://math-www.uni-paderborn.de/HTML/Dictionaries.html

A super list of links to online word dictionaries, foreign language works, hacker's and computer dictionaries, acronym finders, and thesauri. Includes links to such classics as *Learn How to Swear in German* and *The Devil's Dictionary*.

One-Look Dictionary
http://www.onelook.com/

Forget paging through several specialized dictionaries looking for a definition of that word that has you stumped. One-Look, an online search system, will thumb through more than 50 specialized and general reference dictionaries for you in one mouse click.

Oxford English Dictionary
http://www.oed.com

The classic *Oxford English Dictionary* is going online. Full-text access will eventually require an annual subscription. In the meantime, online trial views and test-drives are offered cost free.

Pedro's Dictionaries
http://www.public.iastate.edu/~pedro/dictionaries.html

This site provides links to obscure terminology dictionaries such as *The Cell Biology Dictionary*, as well as linguist references like *Roget's Thesaurus* and the *Esperanto-English Dictionary*.

Roget's Thesaurus—ARTFL Project
http://humanities.uchicago.edu/forms_unrest/ROGET.html

The public domain, 1991 version of *Roget's Thesaurus*, is searchable online at this University of Chicago site.

A Web of On-line Dictionaries
http://www.bucknell.edu/~rbeard/diction.html

Robert Beard, at Bucknell University, has compiled a behemoth index to online thesauri, dictionaries, and word-related reference books. Brush up on your Xhosa or Swahili using links from this site. Jump from here to the *Profanity Dictionary*, *The Dictionary of London Slang*, or hundreds of other word references.

WordNet
http://www.cogsci.princeton.edu/~wn/w3wn.html

WordNet is a Princeton University Cognitive Science Lab online reference tool that will yield antonyms, synonyms, hyponyms, holonyms, and other lexical variations on any keyword on demand.

The World Wide Web Virtual Library: Linguistic Resources— Language Resources
http://www.emich.edu/~linguist/www-vl.html

The Virtual Library shelf on Linguistic Resources, maintained by the professional linguists' mailing list members at Eastern Michigan University, is a super site for locating dictionaries, translators, acronym directories, thesauri, and foreign language dictionaries that are housed online worldwide.

WWWebster Dictionary
http://www.m-w.com/dictionary

The full-text, official version of *Merriam-Webster's New Collegiate Dictionary*, Tenth Edition, is searchable online as the "World Wide Webster."

Encyclopedias Online

Encyclopedia Britannica—Britannica Online
http://www.eb.com/

Access the classic *Encyclopedia Britannica* in multimedia form from your home computer. Free sample searches are offered online, but to access the full works, a monthly ($14.95) or annual subscription ($150) is required.

The Free Internet Encyclopedia
http://clever.net/cam/encyclopedia.html

Clif Davis and Margaret Fincannon of the Citizen's Internet Empowerment Coalition maintain this impressive effort to categorize resources on the Net in encyclopedic fashion. A passel of frequently asked questions (FAQs), subject-oriented guides, and Net super sites are indexed here.

Internet Reference Desks Online

The Argus Clearinghouse for Subject-Oriented Internet Resource Guides
http://www.clearinghouse.net

Argus Associates maintains this blue-ribbon directory to worthwhile online resource guides—World Wide Web, FTP, gopher, Internet lists—in various subjects. Think of it as a virtual library reference desk.

WWW Virtual Library Project
http://www.w3.org/hypertext/DataSources/bySubject/Overview.html

The WWW Virtual Library Project began in Europe in 1991 under the auspices of CERN, the European birthplace of the World Wide Web. Today, the project represents a master effort to provide hot-linked indexes to subject-specific interest guides housed on the Net.

General Reference Works Online

Travel-Finder Currency Calculator
http://www.xe.net.currency

Need to know how much a Mexican peso is worth in U.S. dollars? Stop-in here to check the current conversion rate of coinage from any country.

United States Postal Service Zip Code Lookup & Address Information
http://www.usps.gov

Need to know the zip-plus-four code of your new publisher? Access it online in the Your Post Office Zip Code Lookup database.

Quotations Online

Bartlett's Familiar Quotations
http://www.cc.columbia.edu/acis/bartelby/bartlett/

The classic book of quotes (1891) as archived online by Columbia University's Project Bartleby, an electronic repository of the classics.

The Book of Famous Quotes
http://www.geocities.com/athens/7186

Haythum Raafat Khalid maintains these pages of his favorite quotations from the wisdom of the ages. A unique and delightful guide to who said what throughout history, searchable by alphabetical order.

Quotation Resources
http://www.starlingtech.com/quotes

Michael Moncur maintains this one-stop reference to Quotes of the Day, Quotes of the Week, and Quote Links to sites worldwide. The links section points browsers to unusual quotation collections on topics like humor, movies, and mathematics.

Quotations Home Page
http://www.lexmark.com/data/quote.html

Stephen Spanoudis of Lexmark, maintains this first-rate database of over 15,000 quotes. The database is fully searchable by author or subject. Special collections include Annoying Proverbs, Sarcasm, Quotes by Women, and Recent (Contemporary) Quotes.

Yahoo! Quotations Page
http://www.yahoo.com/Reference/Quotations/

A super directory to quotation pages and resource sites on the Net from the people at the Yahoo! search service. Follow the links to archives as obscure as the List of Quotations About Libraries & Librarians.

Style and Citation Resources Online

Electronic Sources: MLA Style Citation
http://www.uvm.edu/~xli/reference/mla.html

The Modern Language Association's guide to how to reference World Wide Web sources, e-mail, mailing list messages, and CD-ROMs.

Electronic Sources: APA Style Citation
http://www.uvm.edu/~xli/reference/mla.html

The American Psychological Association's guide to how to reference World Wide Web sources, e-mail, mailing list messages, and CD-ROMs in psychological papers and research.

Online Newsrooms

Media businesses have been merging for years. The news these days is not so much the mergers as it is the trend toward media that historically came from different delivery channels bleeding into one large feed—a feed that is neither TV, nor the Net, nor cable, but increasingly is all of these platforms experimentally combined into a broader vision of one single broadcast channel.

Microsoft Network (the online service) and NBC News (the TV news program) have merged to provide cross-platform delivery of national and international news. TV viewers and cybercruisers get their news these days from MSNBC, a platform that many see as the wave of the future. Other innovations like Web TV blur the line between TV and other broadcast media.

The Internet is causing some media companies to push the envelope on multimedia formatting. RealAudio, a Progressive Networks company that specializes in the development of software and systems that allow sound broadcasts to be archived over the Net, is a sponsor of several audio-based news sites, like National Public Radio. Browsers can read through the NPR archives, or they can listen to RealAudio renditions downloaded from the Web site.

Think of the following directory as a tour map of the new cybernewsroom. Whatever your beat, you'll find that many of the newswire and newsroom centers operating on the Net are great places to snag late-breaking leads or to glean background data on emerging industries and trends.

ABC News Reports
http://www.realaudio.com/contentp/abc.html

ABC News posts late-breaking tidbits every hour on the hour. Search the archives for Peter Jennings' commentaries, ABC TV news hourly updates, or the text from Johnny Holliday's sports coverage. RealAudio software can be downloaded for those who wish to hear their news.

American News Service (ANS)
http://www.americannews.com

The American News Service, a nonprofit enterprise headquartered in Brattleboro, Vermont, distributes selected features free of charge to more than 700 media outlets nationwide. The features of ANS focus on people who are actively working to solve public problems, from the reseeding of Pacific Coast forests, to the revitalization of urban America.

Associated Press (AP)
http://www.latimes.com/HOME/NEWS/APONLINE

AP Online is a service of the Associated Press, an established wire service that provides continuous news coverage from around the globe. Browse through a wealth of information on issues from Wall Street to the baseball diamond.

Business Wire
http://www.businesswire.com

Business Wire is a grade-A newswire service, issued continuously via the Net. Business Wire releases full-text product announcements and profiles on major U.S. corporations, including Fortune 1000 and NASDAQ companies. The Corporate Profiles section allows browsers access to free reports, which include background data and press contact information.

CBS News: Up To The Minute Link
http://www.uttm.com/

CBS News posts newsbreaks, top stories, movie and music reviews, special features, an audio and video archive, and programming information—including links to other CBS ventures like the CBS Radio Network—to this one-stop Web station.

CNN Interactive
http://www.cnn.com/

Cable News Network (CNN), the cable TV news channel, features an array of online news in all categories from lifestyle to technology trends. An archive of news material, quick news quizzes, a video download vault, and network programming information make the site a great one-stop newsstand.

C-SPAN Online
http://www.c-span.org/

C-Span, the cable TV news company, sponsors this companion site, which includes breaking news, hourly features and links from the Washington Journal series, book chapters and audio transcripts from the BookNotes author interview series, K–12 online classroom companion tours, and TV program notes. Message boards support reader/viewer write-ins and discussions.

MSNBC
http://www.msnbc.com

Microsoft Network (the online service) and NBC News have merged to provide cross-platform delivery of national and international late-breaking news. TV viewers and cybercruisers now get their news not from NBC, but from MSNBC, a multimedia platform that many see as the news wave of the future.

National Public Radio (NPR)
http://www.npr.org

Listen to NPR news and commentary using the downloadable RealAudio player. NPR, America's public radio network, archives radio transcripts and feature stories online. Search for local stations or broadcast schedules, or order NPR tapes online. Argue about books, broadcasts, and cultural issues with NPR listeners and celebrities in the Your Turn discussion forum.

PR Newswire
http://www.prnewswire.com/

PR Newswire was established in 1954 to disseminate news to multiple media outlets on demand. Daily news and press releases are archived online on biotechnology, business, finance, technology, healthcare, energy, politics, and entertainment. The Company News On-Call and Archived News sections house archives for background data search on selected companies for reporters who cover specialized beats.

Reuters NewMedia
http://www.reuters.com/

Reuters, the international news wire and media service, posts late-breaking blurbs from around the world to its Web site.

U.S. Newswire
http://www.usnewswire.com

U.S. Newswire is the nation's leading distributor of news on the government and public policy agencies. The day's top news, press releases, and policy statements are archived in full-text form for easy retrieval.

Yahoo! News
http://www.yahoo.com/headlines

Free daily online news links in all categories—Top Stories, Business, Technology, World, Weather, Sports, Entertainment, Politics, Health, and Community— conveniently indexed by Yahoo!, the search site people. An archive allows for an easy search of former top-breaking stories from assorted Web sites.

Custom News and Clipping Services

For writers, free online news feeds are a dream come true. But the Net is still a terribly slow and uncertain creature. While many call it the Information Superhighway, the Information Dirt Road might be a truer metaphor at times. If you're less than eager to go online daily, hunting and pecking through a behemoth maze of electronic pages, you'll be cheered to hear that you no longer have to go out after your news. You can now get a personalized e-mail edition of the daily news delivered to your desktop.

Push technology, the broad idea that drives Pointcast, After Dark Online, Info Beat (previously known as Mercury Mail), and other desktop delivery systems, allows producers to bundle customized news and push it into people's e-mail boxes. It is a trend that holds hot economic promise. Because push systems literally "push" news and entertainment at people via their computer screens, it is a model that turns the news into something that resembles TV channels. That people like to have information preselected and delivered in channels is a fact not lost on TV media moguls, who have perfected the art of doing just that for several decades now.

Think of these news delivery services as channels of preordered information from sports scores to parenting tips. Jane Q. Public gets the morning sports scores delivered by Pointcast, a free push service, when she logs onto her Internet account. Sandwiched between her sports scores is a commercial ad for the latest jogging shoe. It's TV in a text-based form, and it is underwritten by advertising. Mercury Mail and After Dark are also advertising driven.

Desktop news delivery excites media moguls because people like it. The fact that people like it means that the circulation of these kinds of push feeds could swell to significant numbers. Numbers drive advertising. Advertising is what has driven TV—and what many believe will pay for program development on an increasingly commercialized Internet.

If you like to view your news while online, services like Hunter, from the *Los Angeles Times*, allow browsers to bundle preselected news into a personalized Web page once they are online. Crayon is another Web-based news compilation service, but unlike Hunter, Crayon links to a bevy of online newspapers, magazines, and e-zines daily. You must return to Crayon's Web site each day to read the news that has been linked to your specifications. Crayon operates more like a set of organized media browsing bookmarks than a newspaper *per se*. My Yahoo! operates much like Crayon, but it does not allow browsers to specify the publications they want scanned—only the broad news categories.

Free Custom News Services

After Dark Online
http://www.afterdark.com

Download the free After Dark news retriever. Input custom parameters on the kind of news you wish to receive: sports, entertainment, finance, computing news. After Dark will automatically retrieve and deliver the news headlines to you each morning in the form of a continuously running screensaver. The service includes a ticker-tape stock report option also.

Crayon
http://crayon.net/

Jeff Boulter, a Bucknell University computer engineering student, created "Crayon," an acronym for "CReating Your Own Newspaper." Crayon is a Web-based system that lets browsers create their own Web paper by inputting the categories and Web publications they want linked together daily into one personal news report. Browsers return to the site to read the collected lines daily.

Hunter—The Los Angeles Times
http://www.latimes.com/HOME/REGISTER/

Register online for Hunter, a customized news clipping service from the *Los Angeles Times*. Create a profile that tells Hunter what interests you—from books to obituaries—and Hunter will ferret out stories from the last seven days of the *Times* and the Associated Press wire service and post them to the Web for your personal perusal. This is a great service if you crave regional news from the California home front.

InfoSeek—Personal
http://www.infoseek.com

InfoSeek, the master search site, sponsors a free personalized news search service. Register online by inputting keywords across several news categories. Headline news will be delivered to registrants via e-mail.

Info Beat
http://www.infobeat.com

Info Beat provides free desktop delivery of news blurbs in e-mail form. Receive desktop delivery on sports, hard news, stocks, weather, or entertainment.

My Yahoo!
http://my.yahoo.com

Yahoo!, the California search engine people, sponsors this free service that allows Web browsers to select the kinds of news they wish to receive. Specifications can be made for headline news, sports scores, stock ticker reports, weather reports, and announcements of new Web sites. Browsers must return to the Web site daily to read the links gathered there.

Pointcast
http://www.pointcast.com

Pointcast is the pioneering retrieval service that started the push of broadcast news fervor. Download the application for free. Set the parameters for the kind of news you want and how often you want to receive it, and then wait for the headline news to pop up on your computer screen. Delivery feeds come from newspapers, wire services, weather services, and an impressive slew of magazines.

Fee-Based Custom News Services

If you're a writer who regularly covers a special beat, like finance, technology, or health, you may eventually decide that paying for information retrieval is a smart idea. A lot of time-saving background information can be gleaned from the world's existing databases. Free news delivery services are a great way to keep abreast of the headlines, but if you hope to regularly receive full-text articles be prepared to enter into a monthly subscription or pay-per-view arrangement.

Subscription-based services and pay-per-view download systems abound. These custom news services bundle access to thousands of specialized article databases into one central system. Lexis-Nexis is one of the oldest, most comprehensive, and most expensive systems. NewsPage is one of the newest and least expensive systems.

For general use, we favor the low-cost, monthly subscription services offered by the Electric Library or NewsPage. Most custom news services offer free trial subscriptions or allow for free trial headline searches. Take advantage of these offers before subscribing to any one service.

ClariNet—e.News
http://www.clarinet.com

ClariNet of San Jose, California, is the largest and oldest Internet-based news service, with more than 1.5 million subscribers, primarily newspapers, educational institutions, and Internet service providers (ISPs). e.News includes more than 500 categories dedicated to specialized wire and syndicate feeds on topics like women's issues. ClariNet delivers e.News in a newsgroup format (under the clari. hierarchy) to ISPs worldwide.

DataTimes—EyeQ
http://www.datatimes.com/

EyeQ is a leading business news clipping service. The EyeQ database culls information from more than 5,000 sources, including newspapers, professional newsletters and reports, and broadcast transcripts. Searches can be conducted using a who, what, when, and where parameter system. Headline searches are free. Per article charges apply to full-text views and downloads. Fees vary with the type of service selected.

EasyNet—Brainwave
http://www.telebase.com

EasyNet, a service of N2K Telebase, allows for one-stop Telnet search of more than 800 business databases, including DIALOG, Dun & Bradstreet, and DataStar. A pay-per-view or per-download system is used in lieu of a flat-rate subscription. Look for EasyNet to be replaced by a new Web-based information retrieval service, BrainWave, in the near future.

Electric Library
http://www.elibrary.com/

The Electric Library is a blue-ribbon flat-rate archive of general news and information. The library archives 150 full-text newspapers; 900 full-text magazines; two newswires; 2,000 classic books; an encyclopedia, standard reference atlases, and fact books; television and radio transcripts; and 18,000 images from map, photo, and fine art archives. Subscriptions are $9.95 per month.

Lexis-Nexis
http://www.lexis-nexis.com/

Lexis-Nexis began service in 1973 as Lexis, the first full-text legal information retrieval service. In 1979, Nexis was added as a full-text business and professional retrieval service. Lexis-Nexis today supports multiple data retrieval services at varying price structures for businesses and individuals. The Small Business Advisor service <http://www-1.openmarket.com/lexis-nexis/> offers access to 1,000 resources for small and home-based business owners. Articles, company profiles, stock data, and industry news are accessible. The Small Business Advisor charges $1.95–$4.95 per article download.

National Institute for Computer-Assisted Reporting (NICAR)— Data Services
http://www.nicar.org/

NICAR, at the Missouri School of Journalism, provides information and networking assistance to reporters using computer-assisted research tools and techniques. NICAR provides access to specialized government databases, such as the FBI's Uniform Crime Reports, and the Social Security Administration's Master Death Records, on a low-cost basis to working journalists only. Fees vary with the type of services requested.

NewsPage
http://www.newspage.com/

NewsPage is a top-notch business and technology news retrieval and filtering service. More than 20,000 full-text stories from 500 publications and international wire feeds in more than 2,500 business subject areas are filtered through NewsPage's system every day. Browsers can sample news headlines and read story summaries online, but a subscription is required ($3.95–$6.95 per month) to get full-text stories delivered to one's desktop via NewsPage Direct each morning.

San Jose Mercury News—NewsHound
http://www.newshound.com

The *San Jose Mercury News*, America's first print-based paper to go online, offers Newshound, one of the first subscription-based, full-text-retrieval news-fetch services designed for use by a general readership. The monthly fee is $7.95.

Time-Warner Pathfinder—Personal Edition
http://www.pathfinder.com

Time-Warner's super site, Pathfinder, supports a personalized news retrieval and desktop delivery service called the Personal Edition. News is culled from mainstream magazines like *Time, Money, People,* and *Sports Illustrated,* along with more than 50 press feeds. Subscriptions are $4.95 per month, with a two-month trial membership for free.

CHAPTER 6

Reading the Digital Ink:
Electronic Books, Publishers, and Bookstores

If books are your business, or simply your delight, the Internet archives more books, publishing resources, and bookstores than bibliophiles of days of yore could ever have imagined. The e-book, or electronic book movement, takes many forms. One growing trend is the international free library movement—an attempt to archive the classics online in e-text form. The number of literary treasures already converted to digital form and archived at public repositories is astounding. Little-read authors and obscure works, many of them out of print for a century, are being given a second life as downloadable text-files on electronic library shelves.

While librarians and bibliophiles work to preserve the classics, modern-day commercial publishers are scrambling to discover ways to harness the Net to distribute books in a cost-effective and aesthetically pleasing manner. Many digitized book schemes are focusing on ways to preserve the feeling of a printed book, yet harness the interactive aspects of the online environment; the end result is what we call "books that byte back." Open Book Systems (OBS) has pioneered both a philosophy and a method for converting bound books to online multimedia reading adventures. Click in at OBS to read an amazing collection of papers and essays on the e-book movement.

If you're looking for a specialized bookstore—maybe a store that sells rare first editions, or a science fiction specialty shop that carries small press titles—you'll find what you need on the Net. Indeed, while most publishing enterprises are struggling to find a way to make their online enterprises pay, booksellers have harnessed the power of the Net to reach an affluent and literate audience with startling success. More than 200 bookstores worldwide now have electronic storefronts.

Finally, if publishing is your business, this chapter chronicles the best publishing super sites to visit online to keep abreast of industry news and trends. We also review model experimental Web sites that publishers like Simon & Schuster are using to market and sell their titles online.

The Electronic Book Movement— Free Book Repositories

As copyrights expire on classic works of literature, bibliophiles and librarians worldwide are seeking ways to transfer these cultural treasures from print to electronic archives for easy access by the masses. Think of it as the world's largest public library movement.

If you're interested in the electronic text and public online book repository movement, sign up for the Book People interactive mailing list. Book People is an electronic forum for announcing and discussing books as they come onto the Internet in a public-access form. To subscribe, e-mail John Mark Ockerbloom and Mary Mark Ockerbloom at Carnegie Mellon University at <spok+bookpeople-request@cs.cmu.edu> with a note that says you want to sign on with Book People.

Following we chronicle the best super sites and archives for locating and retrieving classic works of literature in e-text form. Be forewarned: Electronic stacks contain an impressive amount of literature. If you're looking for a classic online, from Jane Austen to Edgar Allen Poe, you're sure to find it as well as literary commentary on it somewhere in the e-libraries of this worldwide movement.

American Memory Project—Library of Congress
http://lcweb2.loc.gov/ammem/ammemhome.html

The Library of Congress's National Digital Library archives an amazing array of photos, letters, prints, recordings, and notebooks related to America's greatest moments. Browsers are afforded electronic glances into rare documents from the American literary scene. Archived treasures include interviews from the Federal Writer's Project (1936–1940) and Walt Whitman's notebooks

Banned Books Page
http://www.cs.cmu.edu/People.spok/banned-books.html

An informative essay on books that have been banned from schools, libraries and public reading in the United States and abroad, including *Little Red Riding Hood* and *Tom Sawyer*. Live links lead to the online storage sites of the classic books cited in the essay, a project of Carnegie Mellon University.

Bibliomania (United Kingdom)
http://www.bibliomania.com

Bibliomania, in the United Kingdom, archives forty classic novels, assorted biographical texts, reference works, and poetry. Access British works as academic as *Brewer's Dictionary of Phrase and Fable* or as renowned as Samuel Butler's *The Way of All Flesh*.

A Celebration of Women Writers
http://www.cs.cmu.edu/afs/cs.cmu.edu/user/mmbt/www/
women/writers.html

Mary Mark Ockerbloom has created this amazing online index at Carnegie Mellon University to the biographies, bibliographies, Web pages, and electronic archives of women writers through the ages.

The Internet Public Library
http://www.ipl.org/reading/books/index.html

The Internet Public Library Reading Room is home to more than 4,500 e-books. The online book catalog/database can be searched by author, title, or Dewey classification category. Both fiction and nonfiction are archived. The library also maintains a feature that allows researchers and students to submit an e-mail query to a reference librarian for assistance in searching the Net.

Literary Resources on the Net (The Classics)
http://www.english.upenn.edu/~jlynch/Lit/

Jack Lynch of the English Department at the University of Pennsylvania maintains this collection of links to literature sites, conveniently divided by literary period, from Medieval to twentieth-century Irish literature.

The On-line Books Page
http://www.cs.cmu.edu/web/books.html

This is Carnegie Mellon University's online index to more than 3,000 books or substantial publications in English that are housed in free online repositories for personal or noncommercial use. This is a great jumping-off point into electronic public access book repositories worldwide. Start your master search for e-texts from this site.

Project Bartleby
http://www.columbia.edu/acis/bartleby

Bartelby is Columbia University's mammoth effort to electronically inscribe classic books and poetry in e-text form. The project, spearheaded by Steven van Leeuwen, is named after Bartleby the Scrivner, from Herman Melville's classic short story. Read W.E.B. Du Bois's *The Souls of Black Folk* or plunge into Gertrude Stein's *Tender Buttons*.

Project Gutenberg
http://www.etext.org/Gutenberg/

A grassroots effort by netizen Michael Hart, Project Gutenberg aims to convert 10,000 classic texts into downloadable e-texts by 2001, the thirtieth anniversary of Hart's efforts that began when he input the "Declaration of Independence" into a University of Illinois computer system. More than 1,000 texts have been converted thus far. Drop in for a file transfer protocol (FTP) download on Dostoyevsky, Plutarch, Virgil, or Joyce, or for a peek at classic delights like *The Violet Fairy Book*.

Victorian Women's Writers Project
http://www.indiana.edu/~letrs/vwwp/

This is Indiana University's digital project dedicated to archiving accurate transcriptions of the works of British women writers of the Victorian era, many of them little read outside academic circles.

Wiretap—Electronic Books
gopher: //wiretap.spies.com

Wiretap, a digital gopher-based library archive, houses classic e-texts of every imaginable kind. Works range from Augustine's *Confessions and Enchiridion* to Winifred Kirkland's *The Joys of Being a Woman*. The *CIA Factbooks* and inaugural addresses of the presidents are also stuffed into this amazing collection.

The Electronic Book Movement— Commercial Book Publishers and Projects

Is the future of book publishing paperless? Can you really read a book online? Will e-rights be as important as print rights for royalties? If the future of book publishing is digital, what should a digital book look like? Should it look and behave like a multimedia CD-ROM? Should it look and behave just like a paperbound book, giving people the feeling that they are holding a work of art in their hands?

If ever an industry was plagued by more questions than answers it's the book publishing business these days. Book publishing, as an industry, has historically shied away from modernization. The publishing industry is chock-full of word people. Word people are notorious technophobes.

The success of brand-new online book and literary sites like Amazon.com and *Salon* magazine have convinced many that literary types are online to stay. That being the case, books are being put online also. No two enterprises envision e-books the same way, however.

Bibliobytes is a company that believes that people will buy books in downloadable e-text form. They sell downloadable e-texts from their Web site. Online Book Systems sponsors an impressive Web-based adventure through the pages of what, in their estimation, a proper digitized book should look like.

Microsoft Network's Music Central is making a bold bet that people will read books online, if the books are revisioned into snappy TV-like multimedia serials. MSN is converting Fred Goodman's printed musical history *The Mansion on the Hill: Dylan, Young, Geffen, Springsteen, and the Head-On Collision of Rock and Commerce,* into a serialized multimedia event accessible on the MSN service as an ongoing entertainment feature.

Modern Age Books has pioneered a system of converting computer and reference books into e-docs or electronic documents accessible online that look, feel, and act like the printed McCoy. They refer to their system as an intuitive interface—a technology overlay that preserves the integrity of book design as we literary Luddites know it (and love it).

The Waite Group Press, a computer imprint owned by Macmillan, digitized many of its computer book titles in 1996, releasing them online as teaching texts for their eZone or educational zone, an online just-in-time computer training center. The Waite Group was known for its tutorial-style printed primers. They used this model to spin their books into interactive online tutorials. They now publish books about computers that truly byte back. Readers log onto the eZone Web site and buy a printed tutorial book. The book comes in the mail, the old-fashioned way. Instead of saying "book" on the spine it says "interactive course." The book buyer/student reads the first lesson of the printed book, logs onto the Web site, and completes the interactive lesson module and quiz while online. Students even receive their final grades or course completion certificates from the automated online system. Goodbye Mr. Chips. These are smart books.

Education and technology tomes seem especially prone to digitalization as the Internet and intranets give companies and colleges the ability to spin one previously bound book onto the screens of thousands of individual computer learning stations simultaneously.

Following we list some of the most interesting commercial e-book enterprises. If the e-book trend intrigues you, subscribe to one of the mailing lists where these trends are discussed as a matter of business. The Computer Book Publishing list, EBook, and the Publisher's Marketing Association list (see Chapter 1, "Getting Your Message Out: E-Mail, Mailing Lists, and Electronic Newsletters") host debates on these issues from time to time.

Bibliobytes—Electronic Books
http://www.bb.com/BB.html

Bibliobytes is an electronic book delivery store, open for business since 1993. Wander down the aisles by genre (from adventure to young adult) or flip open the whole catalog. Bibliobytes sells downloadable books, images, sounds, and programs. They have the rights to more than 1,000 titles, which they sell in unbound e-text form.

Modern Age Books
http://www.mabooks.com

Modern Age is a company dedicated to reformatting books into sophisticated electronic packages. They produce the e-doc engine, a system that converts printed books into electronic books or e-docs. E-doc versions retain the integrity of a printed book by maintaining features like page layout, graphic design, and type style. Modern Age has partnered with Microsoft Press and IDG Books to produce their best-selling computer books in e-doc form.

Microsoft Network's Music Central
http://musiccentral.msn.com/

Microsoft's Music Central is turning printed books into online multimedia mini-series. This movement sees books as entertainment and seeks to exploit the TV-like audience possibilities of online cruisers by converting printed books into broadcast packages much like a TV miniseries. Strong online communities exist among the young, the technically inclined, the musical, and sci-fi enthusiasts. Future book-to-multimedia conversions could be expected to target these market segments. Visit here for previews of *The Mansion on the Hill,* a printed musical history conversion.

Open Book Systems (OBS)
http://www.obs-us.com/obs/obshome.html

OBS is a pioneering online publishing firm, headed by Laura Fillmore. Their Kinetic Publishing software system works to convert paper books into dynamic online adventures. They also construct Internet and intranet systems for corporations. Tour through Nicholas Negorponte's *Being Digital* or Colin Hayes's *Paperless Publishing* as OBS presents them to readers in cyberspace with supporting hyperlinks to amplify the concepts.

Waite Group Press—eZone
http://www.waite.com/ezone

The Waite Group Press's tutorial-style books on computer matters, like how to author Web pages in HTML, are no longer one-way reads. Readers become students. Books are laid out as printed tutorials with lesson plans. Readers read the book, then go online where they work their way through progressive reviews, application exercises, and exams. This is a great example of books that look the same—that is, they come in print form in the mail—yet act very differently when an Internet marketing aspect is activated.

Commercial Bookstores

The selling of books is a respectable, gentleperson's business—certainly not a vocation known for its earth-shaking innovations. The industry was understandably shocked, then, when one of the most innovative business ideas of the decade came from a quiet upstart book enterprise founded in Seattle in July 1995.

Jeff Beezos, an ex–Wall Street executive, hit upon an idea that would shake booksellers by their shirttails. He created Amazon.Com, a company that wedded the art of hand-selling books with the technological smarts and distribution potential of the Internet.

Beezos's idea was really quite simple. If much of the cost of operating a bookstore comes from maintaining a physical space and keeping inventory in stock (up to 130,000 titles at a Borders superstore), why not cut costs by eliminating both the physical space and the inventory?

Beezos did just that. He virtually eliminated the overhead of being a bookseller by going online. His capital expenditures weren't on fancy stores or inventory. His expenditures were on a Web site that operates 24 hours a day, allowing people to order their books through an automated online process.

Once the order is received, then and only then, does Amazon order the titles for shipment to the customer directly from the inventory of the publisher or a warehouser. (Except for best-sellers, which they do stock on hand.) Amazon grossed revenues of more than $16 million in 1996. It has yet to turn a profit, however.

Amazon proved that people will buy books online. Their skyrocketing ride to the top of a business that most assumed locked up by superstores has not gone unnoticed. Barnes and Noble and Borders have noticed, along with about 200 other specialty bookstores. Practically everyone has entered the online bookstore melee.

In March 1997, Barnes and Noble opened its door on America Online. Their Web storefront features an online ordering system <http://www. BarnesandNoble.com> that will rival Amazon to the bitter end. Both promise to fill orders rapidly on about 2.5 million titles, including 1 million out-of-print titles. Deep discounts and special promotions mark the bookselling battlefield. Borders, the other bookselling giant, is also scheduled to open an Internet store in the near future.

Locating Bookstores Online

Readers and writers can direct-dial and order even the most obscure books, 24 hours a day, from electronic bookstores. If you're serious about buying books online, or seek a book specialty shop that caters to your biblio-cravings, there are several great online guides.

The Complete Guide to Online Bookstores <http://www.paperz.com/bookstores.html> is a set of over 200 links to bookstores in every conceivable specialty area. Jump from the Guide to the front door of a university bookseller or to the dimly lit cellar shop of an underground European book monger.

The America Bookseller's Association's BookWeb <http://www.ambook.org> houses a Bookstore Directory <http://www.ambook.org/directory> that links to home pages or provides contact information on more than 5,000 bookstores and outlets in the United States and abroad. The directory supports searches by alphabetical order and by type of bookstore. The catalog range runs from African-American specialty stores to women's bookstores.

If you still can't locate what you seek, try the booksellers' index maintained by the BookWire folks <http://www.bookwire.com/index> at *Publisher's Weekly*. This directory allows for searches by type of bookstore. It chronicles options from antiquarian to university bookshops. Use the following directory to selectively browse some of the larger, quirkier, or more infamous bookstores now operating on the Web.

Directory of Online Bookstores

Alternative Books Superstore
http://web-star.com/alternative/books.html

The Superstore, a project of PPC Books. Ltd. of Westport, Connecticut, stocks those harder-to-find books of special interest from small and alternative presses. Browsers can order online or the old-fashioned way. Categories stocked range from abuse and Christian works to titles for the transgendered. Address e-mail queries to <altbooks@aol.com>.

Amazon.Com
http://www.amazon.com

Amazon.Com is the Seattle-based upstart that came from nowhere to corner the online bookselling market. Its site features a searchable catalog of 1.5 million current titles, and even more out-of-print titles. Authors can link with Amazon.Com from their home pages and receive a royalty or percentage kickback on any title they sell through Amazon.Com by direct Web-based link referral.

Barnes and Noble
http://www.BarnesandNoble.com

The Barnes and Noble book super chain offers full catalog searches and ordering online with deep discounts on best-sellers and a host of special book-ordering services and delivery options.

Bibliofind—Rare Books
http://www.bibliofind.com

Michael Selzer, of Great Barrington, Massachusetts, decided it was too difficult for old-, used-, and rare-book lovers to find what they needed, and for book dealers to connect with their customers. Bibliofind matches the two with one electronic snap. Booksellers (currently more than 750 of them) can list their wares online for a fee, and book buyers can search to their hearts' desire in one central online database. If Bibliofind doesn't stock what you seek, leave a message on the Personal Want List. When your book shows up, you'll be e-mailed.

Book Stacks Unlimited
http://www.books.com

Book Stacks, located in Cleveland, Ohio, is a great general neighborhood bookstore, online since 1991. With an inventory of 380,000 titles, their motto "Your local bookstore—no matter where you live," rings true. Browsers can search the catalog by keyword, title, author, subject, Dewey Decimal, or ISBN and place secure orders online.

Cody's Books Online
http://www.codysbooks.com/

Located in Berkeley, California, Cody's is a general bookstore that caters heavily to the academic and technical book markets. If you're looking for professional books in areas like psychotherapy, give Cody's a dial.

Daedalus Books Online
http://www.daedalus-books.com

Mail-order bargain book veterans will recognize Daedulus as the store that's brought them unbeatable bargains on remainder books in all areas at discounts of 50 to 80 percent for many a year now. Daedalus still stands by its motto: "Priceless Culture. Priced Less." Both books and music are offered through a secure online ordering system.

A Different Light
http://www.adlbooks.com/

A Different Light, America's premiere gay, lesbian, bisexual, and transgendered specialty bookstore, with physical branches in San Francisco, New York, and Hollywood, supports a searchable catalog online, secure electronic ordering, schedules of community events, and announcements about new titles and works in progress from the gay and lesbian press.

Publishing and Book Super Sites Online

Everyone agrees: The Internet is so large that trying to find anything on it can be as unpleasant as trying to find the bathroom in a house with 10,000 doors—all of them unmarked. No surprise, then, that industry leaders, like *Publisher's Weekly,* have decided that the best way for publishers to go online and extend their outreach is by building a super site that serves as a friendly gathering place and rest stop toward all bookish points worth a visit.

The following sites, sponsored by different industry leaders, function as clean, well-lighted places along the sometimes dark and rutted Information Superhighway. They are great places to begin your exploration of book publishing on the Net.

Bookport
http://www.bookport.com/welcome/9550

Bookport is a central resource for those in the publishing industry. Features include the Internet Book Fair (a worldwide directory to publishers and booksellers) and The Internet Roadmap to Books. The Roadmap is a graphical index to all types of book resources online, including electronic libraries, book review archives, book fairs, and master resource sites for writers and publishers.

Browsers can sign up for a mailing list service that sends out announcements about new book related resources online.

BookWeb—American Bookseller's Association (ABA)
http://www.ambook.org/

BookWeb archives ABA conference announcements and articles from their informative newspaper, *Bookselling This Week*. The BookEvents section is a great guide to upcoming book fairs, conferences, and conventions. A Bookstore Directory leads browsers to more than 5,000 bookselling outlets worldwide. The Reference Desk archives statistics and facts about bookselling and marketing.

BookWire
http://www.bookwire.com

BookWire is a service of the leading trade magazine, *Publisher's Weekly*. It's a delightful "two-thumbs-up" site. Archives contain book reviews, best-seller lists, author book-signing itineraries, directories to bookstores and publishers online, and links to 1,000 other book resource sites. If you're new to the Net, start here.

Internet Book Information Center (IBIC)
http://sunsite.unc.edu/ibic

The IBIC has served as a navigational compass to book resources online since 1992. It's still a top-notch tour guide to what's hot and what's not in the online literary world. Browse the What's New for Book-Lovers archive for press and news releases. The WWW Virtual Library—Literature, maintained here, is a great guide with master links to Authors, Readers, Online Books & Magazines, Poetry, Publishers, and other book sites.

Midwest Book Review
http://www.execpc.com/~mbr/bookwatch/

The *Midwest Book Review* sponsors this mega-site with reviews, links, and stellar informational leads for publishers, authors, and book lovers. This is a great site for cyberscribes and publishers alike.

Directory of Publishers Online

Book publishers are scrambling to decide what an online site should look like, as well as what function it should serve. Some presses are following the no-nonsense online bookstore model. They are putting their catalogs online with companion direct-order features. Others are experimenting with super sites that combine point-of-purchase catalogs with clever book promotional features.

Because people expect free things in cyberspace, many large publishers are building giveaway schemes into their sites. Books@Random, from Random House, archives free interactive kids' games inside their Suessville site—an area dedicated to Dr. Suess's kids' books. Macmillan, with a strong imprint in Que computer books, is known for its SuperLibrary of more than 1,000 free downloadable software programs.

The Del Rey imprint at Books@Random posts sample chapters of their best-selling sci-fi, fantasy, and adventure books to the Web. To promote *The Golden Compass*, by Philip Pullman <http://www.randomhouse.com/goldencompass>, Random House put three chapters online, posted audio clips of the book (the book boasts a fantasy language and vocabulary), and sponsored online contests. Inside the @Random Health Center, promotional tie-ins include items like a free online questionnaire tied to *Dr. Love's Hormone Book*.

Simon & Schuster, a large book-producing power, has modeled its Web site, SimonSays, after the community reading room, a concept popularized by larger book chains these days. Many think that what people are after online is a sense of community. Book discussion groups are the online tribe of choice for avid readers. No surprise, then, that SimonSays browsers can chat together online in ready-made book discussion forums.

Books@Random
http://www.randomhouse.com/

Random House, with more than 10,000 titles in print (from imprints like Ballantine, Fawcett, and Ivy Books), sponsors this clever site, worth a visit for many reasons besides buying their books. In Seussville, an electronic playground, visitors can play games and chat with the Cat in the Hat. The Health Center promotes a wide array of best-sellers with tie-ins like free excerpts, quizzes, and questionnaires.

Macmillan Publishing USA—Information SuperLibrary
http://www.mcp.com

As the world's largest computer-book publisher, putting out heavy-hitting imprints like Que and SAMS, it's no wonder that Macmillan came online early in the game. The Macmillan super site sports a catalog of imprints (ARCO, Frommer's, and Weight Watchers, to name a few) and an events section that details where and when authors are appearing for chats and signings. The site transcends the bookstore model by housing a free software library and several Internet search tools.

Simon & Schuster—SimonSays
http://www.simonsays.com

SimonSays is Simon & Schuster's vision of a book publisher's Web site. Rather than simply transferring its print catalog to the Web, Simon & Schuster has created an online site where readers can gather to discuss their favorite S&S works and authors in reading groups, chat live with the authors, participate in online readings, read and write reviews, and receive news about new and forthcoming titles.

Locating Publishers Online

Most publishers maintain Web sites. If you write for a living, regularly visiting publisher's Web sites can give you tremendous market insight into book and imprint trends. Some publishing houses post their manuscript subscription guidelines online, or at the very least they may post the name and contact information of their acquisitions editors. A few, especially in the computer and technical markets, advertise for freelancers, such as technical editors, directly from their Web sites. Use the following special directories to locate and browse publishers' Web sites online worldwide.

BookPort—The Internet Book Fair
http://www.bookfair.com/welcome/bookfair/bphome

BookPort sponsors this directory to publishers' Web sites worldwide.

BookWire Index—Publishers
http://www.bookwire.com/index.html

This is *Publisher's Weekly*'s online guide to more than 900 publishers with Web sites worldwide. This directory allows browsers to search for publishers by genre and type of book produced. Authors and agents will find this guide indispensable in helping to locate publishers in selected specialty areas like romance and children's novels.

Publishers' Catalogues Home Page
http://www.lights.com/publisher/

Peter Scott of Northern Lights Internet Solutions sponsors this impressive electronic gateway to publishers worldwide. Browsers search by country, then by the alphabetical name of the publisher proper. Academic, specialty, and general trade presses are all chronicled here.

CHAPTER 7

Writing for the Markets:
Mystery, Romance,
and Others

If you're a writer, and this is your first trip out on the magic modem strings, where should your journey begin? Several super sites serve as navigational maps for beginning cyberwriters. We recommend three general sites from which to launch your initial meandering: Inkspot, the Official Misc.Writing, and the Writer's Resource Center. See the following listings for highlights on what each resource center has to offer newbie writers on the Net.

Where you go after you're oriented will depend on what you're after—both the kind of writing you do and the kind of support or camaraderie that you seek. If you crave other writers to network with about the writing life or the business of publishing, click on the open conference forums or message boards maintained at Inkspot, The WritersNet, The Writer's BBS, or the Well. The conversations you'll find in progress on these bulletin-style message boards will run the gamut from how to break into a market to how to find freelance work online.

If procrastination has you down, or you need to find the personal power to face your creative demons, there is guidance and support galore online. Both the Journal Writing Resource page and the Black on White (BOW) page offer guidance, tips, and networking opportunities for those who seek creative support. The BOW page supports a unique interactive mailing list and pledge program for writers battling procrastination. The Journal Writing Resource page is a treasure chest of resources for those who use their journals, diaries, or daily-writing-exercise formats to develop their creative sides.

Once you've visited the general hot spots online, and you've developed a feel for the lay of the cyberland, jump down to the following market areas to explore writing in the specialized markets of children's literature, journalism, mystery and crime, poetry, romance, science fiction and horror, screenwriting, or technical writing. The chapter concludes with special listings for young and aspiring writers looking for pen pals or places to publish their original works online.

Directory of Writer's Super Resource Sites

Black on White (BOW)
http://www1.minn.net/~haartman/welcome.html

Scott Haartman's helpful resource for writers tackles the problem of procrastination and writer's block. The site includes tips on how to start writing, prepare a manuscript, and establish a workable writer's schedule. A mailing list can be subscribed to chat with other writers.

Bricolage
http://www.bel-epa.com/

Bricolage is sponsored by Bel Electronic Publishing in the United Kingdom and edited by Trevor Lawrence. The site contains a helpful master archive of articles and links to Internet writing, literature, and book resources.

Inkspot
http://www.inkspot.com/

Inkspot provides links and message boards for all major markets. Writers' Forums host topics for beginning writers, provide advice on how to get published, and allow for the posting of announcements of writing-related events and conferences. Back issues of the bimonthly electronic newsletter, "Inklings," are archived here. The site is also a gateway into the WWW Virtual Library on Writing Resources online.

Journal Writing Resources
http://www.spectra.net/~tbyrne/

This master directory introduces writers to the art of journalizing and how to use a personal journal to unlock or sharpen one's creativity. An intensive bibliography and collection of links direct browsers to the best journaling books and creativity-unblocking programs, like the "Artist's Way."

The Official Misc.Writing Web Site
http://www.scalar.com/mw/

This highly recommended one-stop site is maintained by denizens of the misc.writing newsgroup. Resources include frequently asked questions on writing, links to members' pages and e-mail addresses, and recommended readings and sites for newbies to browse.

The Page BBS
http://www.pagebbs.com/

The Professional Authors Group Enterprise (PAGE) maintains this bulletin board and discussion forum space for use by published authors. Member fees are $50 per year.

SFF Net
http://www.sff.net/

If you author, publish, or read sci-fi, fantasy, horror, romance, or mystery, this page is the place to extend your exploration of your genre and Net resources. SFF Net is a private online service that sponsors its own File Transfer Protocol sites, Internet Relay chat channels, mailing lists, and newsgroups for genre enthusiasts and authors. Payment of membership fees of $8.95 per month entitles browsers to a full range of private services.

The Well
http://www.well.com/

The Well, originating from the San Francisco Bay Area since 1985, is one of the world's earliest and most active online conferencing communities. Camaraderie can be found in more than 260 separate electronic conferences. Use the Byline Conference to network with freelance writers. Visit the Books or Poetry Conferences to chat about electronic publishing and e-zine enterprises. The Filmmaking Conference is a great place to hash out an independent production. The $10-per-month membership fee is peanuts compared to the camaraderie most authors receive in return.

The Write Page
http://www.writepage.com

The Write Page is a general newsletter-style directory to writing and reading resources on the Net. The Newsletter section includes articles on writers' rights, getting published, writing for the markets, conferences, contests, authors' pages, and writing workshops. Hot-linked introductions steer writers off into specialty news and listings related to romance, mystery, westerns, sci-fi, and the paper/trade markets.

The Writer's BBS
http://www.writersbbs.com/

This great site (BBS stands for Bulletin Board Service) sponsors open chats and discussion forums, a helpful article archive, and resource links for writers online.

The Writers' Computer Store
http://www.writerscomputer.com/

This is a specialty store that stocks scripting and plotting software, computer hardware, reference materials, and books for those in the writing, film, and interactive media markets. Physical branches are located in Sausalito and Los Angeles, California.

WritersNet
http://www.writers.net

WritersNet, a project of Stephan Spencer, the husband of a writer, supports an Internet Directory of Published Writers and Literary Agents. It also supports an interesting and intelligent series of message boards and discussion forums on topics like publishing, working with agents, and the art of writing.

Writer's Resource Center (WRC)
http://www.comet.net/writersr/

WRC provides a first-class set of master links to writing resources, professional agencies, literary agents, workshops, genres, and reference sources on the Net.

Children's Markets

A great place to begin an exploration of children's writing and literature on the Web is David K. Brown's Children's Literature Web Guide. Brown is director of the Doucette Library of Teaching Resources at the University of Calgary. His specialty and true love is children's books, and his site includes pointers to everything a teacher, parent, child, or author could hope to find in cyberspace. There is even a special review section on movies and television programs based on children's books.

Books for Children & More: An Editor's Site
http://www.users.interport.net/~hdu/index.html

Harold Underdown, a freelance editor of children's books, maintains this first-rate reference site for authors and editors of children's books. A rich article archive provides advice on contract negotiations and helpful hints on breaking into the business.

Children's Book Council (CBC)
http://www.cbcbooks.org/

The CBC is a membership organization for children's librarians, teachers, authors, and publishers. The Web site archives membership information and chronicles the publications and activities of the CBC. The Member's List provides invaluable contact information and manuscript submission policies for children's presses.

Children's Book Publishers
http://www.scils.rutgers.edu/special/kay/publish.html

Kay E. Vandergrift, Rutgers University Library Sciences, has compiled this great resource listing. In addition to pointers to print publishers, Vandergrift has compiled a unique media contact directory that provides details on producers of children's audio, video, and multimedia products.

The Children's Literature Web Guide
http://www.ucalgary.ca/~dkbrown/index.html

This four-star resource center, maintained by David K. Brown at the University of Calgary, features information and links on children's literature, publishers, booksellers, organizations, and Internet activities related to literature and writing. A review section recommends children's literature for parents, kids, and resource specialists or librarians.

Children's Writer Resource List
http://corpernicus.bbn.com/people/PDavis/cwrl.html

Writer and illustrator Peter Davis maintains this great site. His annotated bibliography on Books on Writing/Illustrating Children's Books is an especially rich resource for newcomers to the field. His Web site is also an entertaining look into how authors can use Web sites to showcase their own works and creativity.

Children's Writing Resource Center
http://www.mindspring.com/~cbi

This helpful little oasis is sponsored by the "Children's Book Insider," a newsletter for children's writers. The center houses a chat room and networking message boards for children's writers and illustrators. The archives feature how-to extracts from past "CBI" newsletters. The center also sponsors the Children's Writing mailing list.

HarperCollins Children's Books
http://www.harpercollins.com/kids/

Publisher HarperCollins' Children's Books division sponsors this Web site, The Big Busy House. Visit the Big Busy for an idea of how children's presses are positioning themselves in cyberspace, a land rich with kids. Itineraries of author tours are posted here. Authors can download submission guidelines.

Kids 'n Stuff
http://pages.prodigy.com/childrens_writers/

Children's author Jody Blosser maintains this informative resource center for children's writers. A host of articles and informational pointers to magazines, newsletters, and books in the genre help orient newcomers.

Society of Children's Book Writers & Illustrators (SCBWI)
http://www.scbwi.org/

The SCBWI is a professional membership organization, founded in 1968, for children's authors and illustrators. More than 10,000 members enjoy the benefits of conferences, newsletters, grants, and informational resources put forward by the association. Past bulletins and newsletter features are archived online.

Yahoo! Children's Literature
http://www.yahoo.com/arts/humanities/literature/genres/children_s/

Yahoo!, the search index people, maintains this rich index to children's literature and writing sites on the Web.

Journalism and News Writing

If cyberspace is your beat, or you want to learn to use the Net to research more effectively for news and magazine writing, you'll find a host of helpful resource centers online to nudge you along. Our favorite orientation site for newbies is the Guide to Electronic & Print Resources for Journalists, maintained by Anne Stuart, Senior Editor at *WebMaster Magazine*. The information here is well-organized, crisp, and up-to-date.

The WWW Virtual Library, maintained by John Makulowich, houses a great set of pointers to Schools of Journalism, Awards and Grants, Professional Papers (on new media), and Internet News Search & Alert Bureaus. Stop by here to expand your search into professional resources available online.

If you seek help learning to use the Net, visit Scoop Cyberslueth's Internet Guide, or FacsNet. If you want to chew the news with veteran reporters or scout for freelance or stringer assignments, drop in at the message boards maintained by the Reporters Network.

CyberWire Dispatch—Brock N. Meeks
http://cyberwerks.com:70/1/cyberwire

Veteran reporter Brock Meeks has won critical acclaim for using the Net as a medium to pen and distribute his hard-hitting, opinionated journalism about cyberlife and technology trends. Browsers can subscribe to Meeks's famously opinionated dispatches here.

The European Journalism Page
http://www.demon.co.uk/eurojournalism/

Stovin Hayter, of the United Kingdom, maintains this gateway into news and news research sources from the European world community. A master directory of resource links to Media, Government, and Journalism sites steers reporters into the heart of the transcontinental newsroom.

FacsNet
http://www.facsnet.org/

The Foundation for American Communications sponsors this one-stop newsroom online. Reporters can access search tools, read about top issues, locate experts for interviews, and browse annotated links to some of the best informational sites online organized by beat area.

Guide to Electronic & Print Resources for Journalists
http://www.cio.com/central/journalism.html

Anne Stuart, Senior Editor at *WebMaster Magazine*, maintains this jewel of a directory to news and journalism hot spots, including professional media mailing lists, news groups, networking forums, and Net research tools.

Journalist's Toolbox
http://www.ccnet.com/CSNE/toolbox.html

This site, sponsored by the California Society of Newspaper Editors, features well-organized, extensive links to Journalism, Government, Media, and What's New sites on the Web.

National Institute for Computer-Assisted Reporting (NICAR)
http://www.nicar.org/

NICAR, at the Missouri School of Journalism, provides information and networking assistance to reporters using computer-assisted research tools and techniques. A helpful primer is archived here, along with information on conferences, newsgroups, and mailing lists. Information on the NICAR special newsgroup news.reporter.org is accessible here.

Online Journalist
http://www.online-journalist.com/

San Francisco State University sponsors this one-stop directory to news, commentary, and resources for the cyberpress. Their News section is a great weekly read of excerpts on the top issues affecting new media and online press enterprises. Their Kiosk section of links to online news, magazines, news feeds, student publications, and e-zines is very worth the browse.

Reporter.Org
http://www.reporter.org/

Reporter.Org is a master directory to online news associations and writers organizations. A master search index at this site allows for searches of documents housed at Reporter.Org as well as all the archives for journalism-related Web sites like those maintained by National Institute for Computer-Assisted Reporting (NICAR). Both concept and keyword searches can be conducted.

A Reporter's Internet Survival Guide
http://www.qbs.net/~casey

Reporter Patrick Casey maintains this stellar guide to online reference sites to federal beats, the courts, sports, education, and politics, among other topics. It's an easy-to-use system of helpful indexes to online information repositories.

Reporters Network
http://www.reporters.net/

The Reporters Network is a blue-ribbon project by Bob Sablatura, reporter for the *Houston Chronicle*. The Network maintains a Media Directory for online journalists; Bulletin Boards for networking, industry news, and jobs; and free e-mail accounts for the working press.

Scoop Cybersleuth's Internet Guide—Journalism
http://www.evansville.net/courier/scoop

Scoop Cybersleuth of the Evansville, Indiana, *Courier Journal* has organized links to many great search sites and key informational centers. His Journalism links are a good starting point for an orientation to reporting sources in cyberspace.

Society of Professional Journalists (SPJ)—The Electronic Journ@list
http://www.spj.org

SPJ is the largest professional organization for members of the working press. Their Web site supports archives on ethics in journalism, "PressNote" industry newsletter, Freedom of Information on the Net, awards and fellowships, and professional development.

World Wide Web Virtual Library—Journalism
http://www.cais.com/makulow/vlj.html

John Makulowich's blue-ribbon master directory to broadcast, journalism, media, and news sources on the Web.

Mystery and Crime Markets

Our favorite one-stop search site for mystery and intrigue on the Net is the Mysterious Home Page, a super directory maintained by Jan Steffensen, of Aalborg, Denmark, with a mirror site located in the United States to make the page easier to access during peak Net traffic hours. This site is a four-star guide to everything mysterious—from international author's conferences to interactive games of intrigue.

When you're done at the Mysterious Home Page, click on over to the Northern California Mystery Writers' pages. The Resource section here provides a well-mapped road into specialized forensic and crime sites online.

The American Crime Writers League (ACWL)
http://www.klew.com/acwl.html

The ACWL is a membership association for crime and suspense writers. Members' biographies, industry news, and membership information are archived online. Links are provided to crime, private investigation, and forensic sites.

The Armchair Detective
http://www.booksellers.com/armchair_detective

The Armchair Detective is a print magazine that publishes articles, book reviews, and author interviews in the mystery genre. The Web site gives subscription information.

Crime Writers of Canada (CWC)
http://www.swifty.com/cwc/cwchome.htm

CWC is Canada's professional crime writers' association. Information is housed here about CWC, its members, and their projects, along with information on industry awards and trends in Canada.

Internet CrimeWriting Network (ICWN)
http://hollywoodnetwork.com/Crime/profile.html

Martin Roth, veteran crime writer, producer, and author, hosts the ICWN. It provides an array of articles and interviews about writing in the crime genre for print, TV, and big screen productions. The Inner Circle is a fee-based membership association for crime writers. The Bullet-In-Board is a message forum for crime writers.

Mysterious Home Page
http://users.aol.com/bchrcon97/mysteris.htm

This Danish center is the cream of the crop when it comes to mystery and intrigue on the Net. A series of original online primers provide a rich orientation to prominent themes in the genre. Links cover all forms of mystery and suspense media, including TV and film noir. European and North American resources are fully chronicled.

Mystery Connection
http://emporium.turnpike.net/%7Emystery/

A great collection of links points browsers to master sites online. Information is provided on "Over My Dead Body," the mystery BBS (bulletin board service) and magazine. "The Magnifying Glass," a monthly newsletter for mystery fans, can be subscribed to here.

Mystery Net
http://www.mysterynet.com/

Newfront Communications, an interactive mystery publisher, maintains this resource center. Mystery Net posts three new mysteries online each week, sponsors solve-it-via-e-mail crimes, and holds contests. Browse the History of the Mystery, a fun interactive tutorial. Read about the latest Anthony and Shamus mystery-award winners. The site also houses a great Mystery Bookstore Directory.

Mystery Writers of America (MWA)
http://www.bookwire.com/mwa/

The MWA has been America's leading membership association for mystery, crime, and suspense writers since 1945. Information is archived on membership, regional chapter activities, and award programs.

The Mystery Zone
http://www.mindspring.com/~walter/mystzone.html

The Mystery Zone is a Web magazine or e-zine for mystery authors and aficionados edited by mystery writer Walter Sorrells. The site archives author interviews and book reviews, along with an impressive collection of links to related crime, suspense and mystery sites.

Northern California Mystery Writers
http://user.aol.com/mwanorcal/index.html

Mystery writers in Northern California have banded together to produce this model grassroots site. Though intended for writers in California, the site is a resource jewel for anyone in the genre. The Resources for Mystery Writers section is one of the best on the Net. Links are provided to crime and forensic research sites, publishers, bookstores, and writing resources on the Web.

Sisters in Crime
http://www.books.com/sinc/home.html

Sisters in Crime is a membership association dedicated to promoting women in the industry and to combating misogyny in both the genre and the publishing world. Authors, agents, booksellers, and librarians are invited to join. Membership information is archived online.

Poetic Markets

The Net is rich in academic poetry archives, experimental poetry e-zines, and grassroots coffee houses and networking forums. No matter your poetic tastes, from the Canonical verse of centuries gone by to the current group slams and free verse, the Net has a poetic niche for you.

Begin your academic quest at the Electronic Poetry Corner (EPC). The EPC provides hot links to authors, magazines, small poetry presses, Internet mailing lists, and poetry archives and activities hosted on the Net. EPC is a great resource if you're scouring cyberspace for vibrant new journals or the latest information on computer-generated poetry texts.

If you're looking for places to post, publish, or exchange your poetry online with other lyrical souls, click in on the Yahoo! forum directory for leads to online poetry workshops and electronic chapbook projects. The Live Poet's Society is a great place to read original new works online and to upload your own ditties. JStarr's Poetry Forum is a great place to wax poetic with a veritable electronic tribe.

Academy of American Poets
http://www.poets.org/

The Academy, founded in 1934, is America's largest association dedicated to the appreciation of poets, their publishers, and their literary audience. The Academy sponsors National Poetry Month, poetry readings and residencies, and prizes and awards for poets. Information on membership and activities is archived online.

The Atlantic Monthly's Poetry Page
http://www.theatlantic.com/atlantic/atlweb/poetry/
poetpage.htm

The Atlantic Monthly sponsors this monthly multimedia adventure into poetry and poets, both classic and contemporary. Download from an Audio Anthology of poets reading their work as published in the print edition. Raid their archives for classic tidbits from the history of American poetry through the essays and letters of the time.

The CMU Poetry Index of Canonical Verse
http://english-server.hss.cmu.edu/poetry

Carnegie Mellon University sponsors this site of canonical verse, from Maya Angelou's "Inauguration Poem" to William Wordsworth's *Complete Poetical Works*. CMU also electronically publishes *Sudden,* an original poetry journal that invites e-mail submissions.

Database of African-American Poetry
http://etext.lib.virginia.edu/aapd.html

The University of Virginia's Electronic Text Center sponsors this database, based on an anthology of more than 2,500 poems from William French's *Afro-American Poetry and Drama: 1760–1975.*

Electronic Poet's Corner (EPC)
http://wings.buffalo.edu/epc/

EPC is a service of the Poetic's Department of the University of Buffalo. This great resource archives poetry, posts academic information, and provides pointers to other poetic niches on the Web.

The Internet Poetry Archive
http://sunsite.unc.edu/dykki/poetry/home.html

Sponsored by the University of North Carolina Press and the North Carolina Arts Council, this archive houses the works of eight living poets from around the world, including Nobel Prize winners Seamus Heaney and Czeslaw Milosz. The archive includes audio presentations.

JStarr's Poetry Forum
http://www.wolfnet.com/~jstarr/poetry/

JStarr's is an electronic tribe or community of poets. Members post original works to the online archive, participate in online discussion forums, and pitch in to provide inspiration and critiques concerning works in progress.

The Live Poet's Society
http://www.catalog.com/cgibin/var/bartmon/welcome.htm

The Society, a project of poet Linda Bartmon, features the grassroots poetry of more than 800 cyberscribes. Live Poets continually accepts new poetry into its growing archives. An audio archive of poems is also available. Links and information on contests, competitions, and the poetic life abound. Poets can query each other in the message forums.

Poets & Writers Online
http://www.pw.org/

The magazine *Poets & Writers* sponsors this Web site with information for poets and writers as well an open chat board, The Speakeasy. A part of their printed

Directory of American Poets & Fiction Writers is searchable online, providing contact information for more than 2,800 poets and other writers.

Representative Poetry Index
http://library.utoronto.ca/www/utel/rp/indexdates.html

This impressive index of more than 1,340 English poems from the early medieval period to the twentieth century is maintained by the University of Toronto.

San Francisco State University's Poetry Center
http://www.sfsu.edu/~newlit/links.htm

This is a great central link site for exploring poetry on the Net. Links are provided to literary resources, electronic archives, poetry presses, literary journals, world-wide poetry pages, and poets' pages.

Yahoo! Poetry Online Forums
http://www.yahoo.com/Arts/Humanities/Literature/Genres/ Poetry/Writing/Online_Forums

A great search index with pointers to scores of online poetry cafes, innovative online chapbook projects, and lyrical meeting places.

Romance Markets

Romance writers ink out almost half of all paperback books sold in the United States each year. With love and lust such a booming business, it's no wonder a slew of online sites currently compete to woo the romance writer and reader.

Romancing the Web is a great place to start your online romantic meanderings. The site includes authors' pages, book reviews, a newsletter, master links to romance Net resources, a bookstore (with used and new offerings), and online message boards.

If you want to meet other romance authors and learn the tricks of the trade, stop by RomEx—Dueling Modems. This master site promises to be a first-class Web forum for the love forlorn. If you've still not had enough heartbreak, hop over to *The Literary Times* and join in on a message board discussion about romance book marketing.

Canadian Romance Authors Network (CRAN)
http://www.islandnet.com/~dtsi/cran.htm

CRAN is a professional networking association for Canadian romance writers. The site includes a member roster, an electronic newsletter, and an active bulletin board for discussing romance writing, marketing, and book publishing.

Erotic Reader's Association (ERA)
http://www.elite.net/~natsasha/era/

ERA is a membership association dedicated to the online study and discussion of the erotic in musical, movie, and literary forms. Both men and women are welcome.

The Literary Times
http://www.tlt.com/page2.htm

The Literary Times is a national publication that carries features, articles, and reviews for the romance market. The Web site supports author chat forums, electronic book signings, writers' guidelines, message networking boards, and a great how-to article archive.

Romance Novel Database
http://www.sils.umich.edu/~sooty/romance/

Christina Powell of the University of Michigan maintains this rich database of reviews on romance literature, primarily the Regency, and historical works like *Fancy Pants* and *The Bride Wore Spurs.* The database can be searched by title, author, subgenre, or book rating.

Romance Novels & Women's Fiction: A Reader's Guide
http://www.sff.net/people/ValerieTaylor/

Archived at the SFF Net site, Harlequin Romance novelist Valerie Taylor's guide is a great one-stop compass to sites of interest to those who read, write, critique, or collect in the romance genre. The site contains annotated links to authors' home pages (Yes, Fabio has one too!), publishers, bookstores, and discussion groups.

Romance Writers of America (RWA)
http://www.rwanational.com/

RWA is a leading professional association for romance writers and publishers. The site houses membership information, award announcements, and industry information.

Romancing the Web
http://www.romanceweb.com/

The site includes author's pages, book reviews, a newsletter, master links to romance Net resources, a bookstore (with used and new offerings), and online message boards. Romance authors can arrange, for a fee, to have their own Web pages housed here.

Romantic Times Magazine
http://www.rt-online.com/

Romantic Times, the monthly magazine, is considered by many to be "the" definitive source of industry news and events. The site includes a back-issues archive, a romance-writing bookstore, romance writer awards lists, book reviews, and a Writer to Writer feature for romance writers looking to network online.

RomEx Forum—Dueling Modems
http://romex.dm.net/forum.html

RomEx is the active grassroots romance writers and readers forum. Message boards, chats, archives, member bios, and free networking space are offered online.

Science Fiction, Fantasy, and Horror Markets

If you're looking for the best jumping-off point online for science fiction resources, try Chaz Boston Baden's Science Fiction Resource Guide housed at Rutgers University. This guide is a master directory to what's where on the Net, from chat channels to publishers, to interactive games and serialized electronic novels online.

Dominion—The Sci-Fi Channel Online
http://www.scifi.com

The Sci-Fi TV Channel sponsors this four-star Web site for enthusiasts. In addition to program listings and general information, the Dominion sponsors a Seeing Ear Theatre that archives downloadable audios of classics like Orson Welles' *The War of the Worlds* and classic TV shows like *Dimension X*.

HorrorNet
http://www.horrornet.com

A one-stop shop with an authors' directory, publishers' index, book reviews, industry news, and information for horror writers.

Horror Writer's Association (HWA)
http://www.horror.org

HWA is America's membership association for authors working in the horror and dark fantasy genre. HWA sponsors the Bram Stoker Awards each year. Membership information and frequently asked question (FAQ) files for new writers are archived online.

Science Fiction & Fantasy Writers of America (SFWA)
http://www.sfwa.org/

SFWA is America's premiere membership association for authors in the sci-fi and fantasy genres. Membership information is archived here. The site is a super place for exploring the sci-fi genre. Informational pointers are provided to publishers, online hangouts, and writing resources. A host of helpful how-to and contract-negotiation articles are archived here also.

Science Fiction Resource Guide
http://sflovers.rutgers.edu/Web/SFRG/

This master site points browsers to what's housed where on the Net. Industry awards, authors' pages, literature archives, conventions, bibliographies, chat channels, mailing lists, games, TV pages, fan clubs, author FAQs, e-zines, Usenet groups, and more are detailed in this directory.

Science Fiction Weekly
http://www.scifiweekly.com/

This is a great weekly online sci-fi magazine that includes industry news, literary pieces, Hollywood and TV tidbits, an archive of back issues, online links, and games. Submissions are accepted via e-mail.

SF Canada—Speculative Writers' Association of Canada
http://sfhelios.physics.utoronto.ca:8080/sfchome.html

Canada's membership and outreach organization for professional sci-fi and speculative writers. Information is provided on membership, author activities, awards programs, and industry events.

Science Fiction and Fantasy Round Table on the Web (SFRT)
http://www.sfrt.com/sfrt2.htm

This is a great master directory and resource center from the Dueling Modems online service. Information is archived on members, conferences, publishers, and a lively discussion board that allows browsers to chat with other writers and sci-fi, horror, and fantasy fans.

Yahoo!—Science Fiction, Fantasy, Horror
http://www.yahoo.com/Business_and_Economy/Companies/
Books/Science_Fiction_Fantasy_Horror/

This site contains well-organized links from Yahoo! to the best sites related to all aspects of the genre online.

Screen, Script, and Playwriting Markets

Our favorite places to launch screen, play, and scriptwriting searches on the Net are Charles Deemer's Screenwriters and Playwrights Home Page and the European master site, Screenwriter's Heaven. Both super sites are updated regularly, providing intelligent pointers to what's new and noteworthy on the Net.

If you're looking for honest how-to primers, stop by Screenwriter's Utopia or the Screenwriter's Home page. Both are no-nonsense repositories of information about breaking into the business and continuing to thrive once you've got your foot inside the great movie machine.

Drew's Scripts-O-Rama
http://pobox.com/~drew/nontable.htm

The most comprehensive repository of free film scripts on the Net. Those studying the nuts-and-bolts of scriptwriting will find this site a godsend. Draft, shooting, and production versions are archived.

Internet Screenwriter's Network
http://Screenwriters.com/hn/screennet.html

This busy resource center is a good one-stop site. Chat rooms cater to screenwriters. To become a member, and receive extended access to specialized services, one must have written at least one script. There are no member fees.

Playwrights Union of Canada
http://www.puc.ca

This site contains a database of plays, a catalog of books, membership information, industry and contract news, and a Who's Who Directory to the Canadian drama community.

The Playwriting Seminars
http://www.vcu.edu/artweb/playwriting/

Richard Toscan of Virginia Commonwealth University maintains this "opinionated Web companion on the art and craft of playwriting." On the Web since 1995, this 210-page instructional guide is the first arts and humanities text published entirely on the Net. This is a pleasurable must read for dramatic writers of all stripes, including film and screen adapters.

Screenwriter's Heaven
http://www.impactpc.demon.co.uk/

The United Kingdom super site sports frequently asked questions (FAQs) files, European workshop and open-competition information, a script library (which houses drafts, directors' versions, and shooting scripts), virtual-writing workshop announcements, and scriptwriting software reviews accompanied by pointers to downloadable demos.

The Screenwriters Homepage
http://home.earthlink.net/~scribbler

This is screenwriter Brad Mirman's helpful down-to-earth resource with columns on screenwriting, interviews with working authors, news from the big screen and the little screen, and useful tips on pitching your ideas to the Hollywood movie machine.

Screenwriters Online
http://www.screenwriter.com/insider/main.html

Screenwriter Lawrence Konner maintains this master site with access instructions into a live chat room (#screenwriters), interviews with writers, sample subscriptions to *The Screenwriter's Insider Report,* and a writer's calendar of international conferences and events.

Screenwriters and Playwrights Home Page
http://www.teleport.com/~cdeemer/scrwriter.html

Charles Deemer, veteran playwright and instructor, maintains this master directory to screen, script, and playwrighting information online. Pointers are provided to FAQs, movie reviews, movie databases, script archives, conferences, and how-to resources on the Net. Information on accessing the Green Room chat center for playwrights and screenwriters is also housed here.

The Screenwriters Utopia
http://www.screenwritersutopia.com

This resource center, created by Christopher Wehner, archives author interviews, industry news, how-to columns, message forums, and other things that would interest any and every aspiring writer in the field.

The TV Writer Home Page
http://home.earthlink.net/~lbrody/indexaa.html

This is a great real-life advice page on writing and producing for the TV markets, including animated and comic series, by Larry Brody, a writer with credits from *Star Trek, Hawaii Five-O,* and other prominent series. Brody's site houses sample scripts, reviews of scripting programs, his own downloadable scripting template, and a FAQ file.

Writers Guild of America (WGA)
http://www.wga.org/

WGA is a membership and employment guild for professional writers, primarily those working in film, broadcast TV, and multimedia and game scripting areas. The Guild publishes guidelines for freelance-writing conditions and fees. Helpful articles cover the screen and scripting industry.

Yahoo! Screenwriters' Resources
http://www.yahoo.com/Entertainment/Movies_and_Films/
Screenplays/Screenwriter

A great one-stop search site for commercial and non-commercial screen and script sites on the Web.

Technical Writing Markets

Technical writers author technology-related books, pamphlets, reports, and manuals. They compose or edit computer manuals, technical reports, multimedia presentations, and manuals for engineering and scientific disciplines. In addition to visiting the following master resource sites, some great places to network with others of this ilk include the Computer Book Publishing list, maintained by Studio B <http://www.studiob.com>, or the Techwr-L mailing list <http://www.documentation.com/techwrit/techwrit-l.htm>.

Internet Resources for Technical Communicators (Soltys)
http://www.interlog.com/~ksoltys/techcomm.html

Keith Soltys maintains this great central search site to technical books, writing resources, and Internet networking clubs for technical communicators. There is an good list of mailing lists for technical and computer writers.

Internet Resources for Technical Communicators (Perez)
http://www.rpi.edu/~perezc2/tc.index.html

Cris Perez maintains this exemplary resource site that details mailing lists, newsgroups, and journals for technical writers.

John December Technical Communication Information Sources
http://www.december.com/john/study/techcomm/info.html

Author and teacher John December maintains this first-class site that contains a wealth of informational links about online writing and communications projects. The site is also an excellent example of an author-maintained promotional effort.

Society for Technical Communication (STC)
http://stc.org/

The STC is the world's largest membership organization for technical writers, editors, publishers, and illustrators. Membership, publication, and career resource links and information are provided in this site.

Technical Communications Resources
http://www.in.net/~smschill/techcomm.html

Stephen Schiller had developed this master site of supremely useful resources. Detailed links exist to job opportunities, training, industry connections, writing resources, and magazines in the field. An impressive one-stop shop.

Technical Writing
http://user.itl.net/~gazza/techwr.htm

Gary Conroy, a British computer analyst and programmer, maintains this top-notch center for technical writers. The center includes an introduction to the career area and links to a fistful of online writing resources.

Young Writers Online

If you have budding young writers in the house, hook them up to other young writers on the literary scene by visiting the following young writers clubs online.

Cyberkids—Cyberteens
http://www.cyberkids.com

Cyberkids sponsors an online reading room and writing contests for young authors. A companion Cyberteens site is rich with original writings and projects for teen authors.

Kidworld
http://www.bconnex.net/~kidworld

Kidworld accepts submissions from anyone under 16. The online site features a chat board and a worldwide pen pal program for young writers.

Little Planet
http://www.littleplanet.com/

Little Planet is a great little kid's cyberpaper that accepts original stories and artwork by e-mail from children worldwide.

Quill Society
http://www.quill.net/

Quill is an active membership society for writers ages 12–24. The society sponsors a chat room, message board, mentoring program, discussion mailing list, story archive, and a monthly newsletter.

Stone Soup
http://www.stonesoup.com/

Stone Soup is the first national magazine for children which is also primarily written and illustrated by children ages 8–13. Sample issues, submission guidelines, and projects are archived online. A Pen Pal feature unites young writers and artists.

CHAPTER 8

Networking and Rubbing Electronic Elbows: *Agents, Authors, and Professional Associations*

Once upon a time, if you needed an agent, you had to trudge down to the village library to see if they had a copy of the *Literary Market Place* or another master guide to literary agents. The Internet is changing all this. While the majority of agents are not yet online, master directory projects like LiteraryAgent.Com and The Internet Directory of Literary Agents aim to make locating an agent as simple as firing up your modem and taking a trip out onto the World Wide Web.

Many authors are finding that hosting their own Web pages with samples or excerpts from their published works is a good way to promote themselves and make their expertise known to a larger audience. In an effort to take advantage of the low-cost promotional possibilities of the Internet, many authors, as well as agents are hosting their own Web pages and taking the time to enter their talents into master online directories like the WritersNet: Internet Directory of Published Writers.

Writing is by nature a solitary occupation, but the Internet is making it much easier for authors to link-up to discuss issues related to professional development. The Internet houses a treasure chest of information on professional associations that specialize in helping authors to connect and network with each other. The last part of this chapter highlights professional associations, like the Education Writers Association and the National Association of Science Writers, that specialize in linking together authors who might not otherwise meet.

General Directories of Agents and Authors

AuthorLink!
http://www.authorlink.com

AuthorLink! is an online repository that markets ready-to-publish works to agencies and acquisition editors. The site supports a directory of literary agents.

LiteraryAgent.Com
http://www.literaryagent.com

LiteraryAgent.Com is a joint project of the Mesa Group (publishers) and Proteus Designs (book designers). The database yields contact information for agents with Web pages as well as agents without Web pages or e-mail addresses.

WritersNet: Internet Directory of Literary Agents
http://www.writers.net/agents.html

This master directory is restricted to agents who do not charge reading fees. Authors can browse listings by name, agency, country, or specialty. Agents can add their own listings for free.

WritersNet: Internet Directory of Published Writers
http://www.writers.net/

The WritersNet database of published writers is maintained by Stephan Spencer. Browsers can search by type of writing or alphabetical name entry. Published writers can add their entries for free.

Yahoo! Authors
http://www.yahoo.com/arts/humanities/literature/authors

An easy-to-use index to authors' home pages and projects on the Web. This index will turn up the literary archives of deceased masters as well as the home pages of contemporary authors. Once there, browsers can sub-sort in categories from the Beat Generation to the Victorian Era. Mystery, sci-fi, and other markets are listed here, too.

Children and Young Adults

Inkspot: Children's Author & Illustrator's Directory
http://www.inkspot.com/author/directory.html

A master directory to the Web pages of contemporary children's authors and illustrators.

Computer Books

Studio B Productions—Computer Book Cafe
http://www.studiob.com

Studio B is a literary agency and custom publisher of computer books. It sponsors the Computer Book Publishing list. The Computer Book Café archives articles of interest to those who write for computer-related markets.

Waterside Productions
http://www.waterside.com

Waterside is a leading agency specializing in the representation of computer book authors. Selected nonfiction in business, reference, health, sports, psychology, and how-to titles are also accepted for representation. Waterside hosts an annual computer book publishing conference in San Diego, California.

Journalism

Directory of Investigative Journalists
http://www.ire.org/resources/journalists/

Investigative Reporters & Editors (IRE) sponsors this national directory of reporters. Entries include phone numbers and agency affiliations.

Reporter's Network—Media Directory
http://www.reporters.net/

The Reporter's Network maintains this master e-mail directory of online reporters and journalists. Reporters can be searched for by name, specialty, or news affiliation.

Mystery and Crime

The American Crime Writers League (ACWL):
Member Personal Web Sites
http://www.klew.com/acwl.html

The ACWL is a membership association for crime and suspense writers. Members' personal Web pages are archived in this directory.

Crimewriter's Directory
http://hollywoodnetwork.com/Crime/directory.html

Crimewriters.com sponsors this directory of biographical information, e-mail addresses, and Web page links for crime and mystery writers, many of them working in film.

The Mysterious Home Page: Personal Mystery Homepages
http://www.db.dk/dbaa/jbs/pershome.htm

Jan B. Steffensen of Denmark maintains this first-rate index to the home pages of contemporary mystery writers from the United States and abroad.

Romance

Romance Novelist's Directory
http://www.comet.chv.va.us/writerhp.htm

This directory provides links to the Web sites of contemporary romance authors.

Science Fiction, Horror, and Fantasy

SFF Net—Science Fiction, Horror, Fantasy Agents
http://www.sff.net/sff/agents.htp

The SFF Net master Web site sponsors these listings and links to agents that specialize in the genre markets.

SFF Net—Science Fiction, Horror, Fantasy Authors
http://www.sff.net/sff/aut_page.htp

The SFF Net master Web site maintains these annotated links to the home pages of genre authors online.

Screen, Script, and Drama

HollyDex: Hollywood Access Directory
http://Screenwriters.com/Directory/index.html

A project of the Hollywood Network, HollyDex aims to become the definitive online directory to agents, consultants, and producers who specialize in screen, script, or multimedia deals.

Playwrights Union of Canada—Who's Who
http://www.puc.ca

This site supports a master directory of Who's Who on the Canadian drama scene.

The Screenwriters Homepage—Agents List
http://home.earthlink.net/~scribbler/agency.html

A directory of agents who handle screen and script materials from the Writer's Guild of America (WGA) can be found here.

Screenwriters Nebula Drive
http://users.aol.com/blcklab666/home.html

Nebula Drive is a repository for industry news and links to related sites. A database houses profiles of screen and TV writers online. Writers are listed by genre with e-mail and home-page hot links.

Professional Associations

Joining a professional association is a great way to gain insider's information into your chosen writing market. Many professional associations, like the Society of Professional Journalists, sponsor academic fellowships and annual conferences. Some, like the National Endowment for the Arts, actively award grants to new artists and authors.

To keep up to date on associations of interest to writers, including those that do not maintain Web sites, visit the online directory of Associations and Organizations of Interest to Writers <http://www.azstarnet.com/~poewar/ writer/associations.html>. This great site details surface mail information on writing-related organizations in the United States, Canada, and abroad.

We detail the following professional associations of interest to writers who maintain Net sites or online archives. If you write primarily for the fiction markets, such as mystery or science fiction, see Chapter 7, "Writing for the Markets: Mystery, Romance, and Others," on market writing, for information on the professional associations (like the Mystery Writers of America [MWA]) that serve these special markets.

American Society of Newspaper Editors (ASNE)
http://www.asne.org/

ASNE is a professional standards and networking association for editors and publishers. Publications, resources, and industry news and events are archived online. The results of surveys on the news room and new media enterprises are also archived here.

Associated Writing Programs (AWP)
http://www.gmu.edu/departments/awp/

The AWP is a nonprofit organization dedicated to fostering creative literary talent nationwide and in colleges and universities. The page includes information on the annual AWP conference, funding projects, awards programs, a guide to AWP creative writing programs, and information on members' benefits, including a job placement list.

Association of Teachers of Technical Writing (ATTW)
http://english.ttu.edu/ATTW/

ATTW is an international membership association of 1,000 teachers and professional communicators who work in the area of technical and computer-assisted communication. News, online resource links, academic syllabi, journal abstracts, a Net mailing list, and membership information are archived online.

Bibliographic Society of America (BSA)
http://www.cla.sc.edu/engl/bsa/

The BSA is an academic society that promotes bibliographical research and publications. The page includes membership information, grant and fellowship bulletins, society paper and book announcements, and related links.

Education Writers Association (EWA)
http://www.ewa.org/

EWA is a professional organization for education reporters, writers, and editors. Membership, conference, fellowship, and professional-development resources are archived here. Award-winning educational stories are also featured.

Electronic Frontier Foundation (EFF)
http://www.eff.org/

The EFF is the American Civil Liberties Union of the Internet. The nonprofit organization works to shed light on free speech and access issues as they relate to the Electronic Frontier. Issues related to copyright, intellectual property, new media ethics, and online privacy are tackled by the EFF. A library archives position papers and articles.

Garden Writers Association of America
http://www.hygexpo.com/gwaa/

The Garden Writers Association is a nonprofit organization for those who write about gardening, horticulture, or landscape architecture markets. The Web site supports a hotlinked list of book and magazine publishers that deal in gardening material as well as informational articles for writers.

HTML Writers Guild
http://www.hwg.org/

This guild is dedicated to providing professional networking and informational services to HTML (Hypertext Markup Language) page authors and Internet publishers. More than 50,000 members worldwide enjoy access to the mailing lists, IRC (Internet Relay Chat) channels, and instructional archives supported by the guild.

International Affiliation of Writers Guilds (IAWG)
http://wga.org/lawg/index.html

IAWG is an international affiliation of screen- and scriptwriters' guilds worldwide. Membership information is archived online.

International Women's Writing Guild (IWWG)
http://www.iwwg.com/

IWWG is a networking and camaraderie association for women writers. A calendar of events, including women's writing workshops and conferences, is archived with membership information online.

The Internet Society
http://www.isoc.org/

The Society is a nongovernmental agency working to promote international Net policies and protocol. Information is archived on issues like cryptography, domain name standards, and international usage and access.

Internet Press Guild (IPG)
http://www.cybernothing.org/ipg/

The Internet Press Guild is a nonprofit organization dedicated to excellence in journalism on online services and the Internet. The Web site serves as a clearinghouse to online resources for journalists. IPG members can subscribe to a private mailing list on Net journalism.

Investigative Reporters and Editors (IRE)
http://www.ire.org/

IRE is a membership association for investigative journalists. Membership information, helpful handouts, conference announcements, and information on the IRE mailing list are posted here. IRE also maintains an online story background resource center accessible on a fee basis or with an annual membership.

Journalism and Women's Symposium (JAWS)
http://www.jaws.org/index.html

JAWS is a nonprofit agency dedicated to promoting the advancement and well-being of women in the newsroom. Scholarship, job, networking, conference, and professional-development information are archived online.

National Association of Black Journalists (NABJ)
http://www.nabj.org/

NABJ is the largest professional association for people of color in the world. Membership information, scholarship and intern information, and journal highlights are archived online.

National Association of Science Writers (NASW)
http://nasw.org/

NASW sponsors this page, which provides information, membership outreach, and resource links for science writers.

National Endowment for the Arts (NEA)
http://arts.endow.gov/

The National Endowment for the Arts Web site is a mega-house of information about the arts in America. Information on NEA grants is housed here, along with a lively assortment of essays, publications, and links to online art agencies. The Writers Corner <http://arts.endow.gov/Community/Writers/wcindex. html> archives works by authors who have received Fellowships from the Endowment's grants program.

National Institute for Computer-Assisted Reporting (NICAR)
http://www.nicar.org/

NICAR is a leading educational association for online reporters. NICAR sponsors a mailing list (NICAR-L) and provides informational primers and pointers on computer-assisted reporting.

National Poetry Foundation (NPF)
http://www.ume.maine.edu/~npf/

Housed at the University of Maine, the NPF was founded in 1972 to promote literary poetry pursuits. The site archives several journals, allows for registration to the Ezra Pound poetry discussion list, and posts blurbs on upcoming conferences.

National Press Club
http://npc.press.org/

The National Press Club is a Washington-based journalist's club for news and debate. The Web site archives political news, class and speakers' schedules, and membership information. Links are provided to online journalistic and news resources.

National Press Photographers Association (NPPA)
http://sunsite.unc.edu/nppa/

NPPA is a membership organization for photojournalists. Membership information, industry news, publications, and educational opportunities are posted to the Web site.

National Writer's Union (NWU)
http://www.igc.apc.org/nwu/index.htm#Contents

The NWU, the trade union for freelance writers, provides labor grievance assistance, an agents database, a publication rights clearinghouse, a Technical-Web-Multimedia Job Hotline, health insurance, press passes, networking, and invaluable materials on emerging issues like contract negotiation for electronic rights.

Newspaper Association of America
http://www.naa.org/

The Newspaper Association of America is a nonprofit agency that looks after the interests of America's $46 billion newspaper industry. The Association deals with issues of marketing, public policy, diversity, and newspaper operations as well as policies and trends in digital publishing. The Web site includes information on conferences, and products and services produced by the NAA for the newspaper industry.

PEN American Center
http://pen.org/

The PEN Center online houses information on its innovative writing programs, including its Freedom-To-Write banned books and authors alert program and the Prison Writing Program. Information on PEN's literary awards and grants programs is also archived here.

The Playwrights Project—The Restoration of American Theatre
http://www.vnet.net/users/phisto/

The Playwrights Project is a nonprofit organization dedicated to providing funding for a writer-dedicated environment in the Carolinas that will sustain up to thirty new playwrights and their emerging productions each year. Links are provided to theater resources on the Net.

Publisher's Marketing Association (PMA)
http://www.pma-online.org/

PMA is the largest trade association dedicated to helping independent publishers succeed in marketing and distributing their audio, book, and electronically published product lines. Information is archived on the "PMA Online Newsletter," annual conferences, the PMA mailing list, and membership.

Pulitzer Prizes
http://www.pulitzer.org/

This is an online directory and informational resource on past and present winners of the Pulitzer Prize, as well as information on current nominees to the Pulitzer in journalism and literary areas.

Society of Environmental Journalists (SEJ)
http://www.sej.org/

SEJ and the International Federation of Environmental Journalists (IFEJ) share this home page of information, job links, conferences, newsletter archives, and resources for environmental journalists.

Society of Professional Journalists (SPJ)—The Electronic Journ@list
http://spj.org/

Founded in 1909, SPJ is a nonprofit association serving more than 13,500 working journalists and editors. The Web site archives a code of ethics, the "PressNotes" newsletter, industry news, fellowship opportunities, and professional development materials.

Writers Guild of America (WGA)
http://wga.org

WGA is the professional guild for screen, script, and multimedia writers. How-to primers and industry news are archived here.

CHAPTER 9

The Online Writery:
Real-Time Chats, Workshops, and Academic Writing Resources

If you've mastered e-mail and the art of posting messages to bulletin boards or newsgroup forums, then you've mastered the Internet realm known as asynchronous communications. *Asynchronous communications* is techno-argot for communicating back and forth with time lapses in between. Internet mailing lists and newsgroup message boards are asynchronous because, while many people "talk" to each other using these systems, they do not talk directly to each other in real time.

It is also possible to use the Internet to talk in real time with multiple users—located across town—even across continents. Systems that allow for real-time chat via your modem are termed *synchronous*. Synchronous means simultaneous. The largest synchronous movement on the Net takes place on Internet Relay Chat (IRC) channels. IRC rooms allow a large number of users to congregate and speak to each other simultaneously. IRC channels are identifiable in print by the "#" sign that precedes them. #Screenwriters, for example, literally means the Screenwriters' IRC channel. Below we list the best Net sites to visit for information on specific clients and chat channels for writers.

To access IRC rooms, you'll need a piece of software called an *IRC client*. The exact type needed will depend on the computer system you use and the specific chat room or channel that you wish to access. A client called mIRC is very popular with Windows users, for example, but it will not work on a Macintosh. The software you will need is generally freely available for download on the Net.

While chat channels are popular with some people, they remain one of the most difficult domains to access on the Net. Most chat clients require users to learn a set of computer command languages. These commands must be typed into the client to access, participate in, and leave chat channels. Learning these commands may seem like learning a foreign language; however, once learned, you may find that you, like many, absolutely love this form of talking live on the Net.

On the up side, some channels now support log-in by more automated software systems. The software used by these systems does away with much of the computer command functions, replacing them with a point-and-click graphical interface.

How Do Writers Use Real-Time Chat?

Writers use chat rooms in three ways. The first is to use them as coffee houses, a place to kick back and commune with other writers. Tight-knit electronic tribes can emerge from such chat channels. This is especially true because the same people tend to come back week after week at the same times to hang with the chosen crowd.

The second way writers are using chat rooms is to provide a real-time, back-and-forth teaching or tutoring environment. Guest lecturers, generally noted authors, may drop in to facilitate a discussion around a set topic. Or, writers may simply meet online at established times to critique each others' works in progress, workshop style. Academic chat rooms are commonly called MAUDs (multi-academic user domains).

Lastly, some writers, especially those in science fiction or fantasy, may use IRC rooms or their direct cousins, MOOs and MUDs (other multiuser, real-time domains), to create gaming or fantasy rooms. MUD stands for multi-user dimension or domain. It can also be read multiuser dialogue. A MOO is a special kind of MUD, and means "MUD, Object-Oriented." In gaming realms, people take on character roles—like Lord of the Dungeon on Planet Zeno. Characters then actively participate in the creation of an ongoing fantasy world.

Directory of IRC Resources

The IRC FAQ
http://www.kei.com/irc.html

If you're new to IRC and online chat rooms, start here. This helpful FAQ (frequently asked questions) lays out the basics so you can get on with the grunt work of locating and installing an appropriate client or software program and logging on. A companion Primer <http://www.kei.com/irc/IRCprimer1.1.txt> provides an excellent introduction to setting up your software, connecting to a server, and using basic IRC line commands. Instructions are provided on where to go online to download the appropriate IRC client for all computer systems: UNIX, MS-DOS, Windows, and Macintosh systems.

IRC—Related Resources on the Internet
http://urth.acsu.buffalo.edu/irc/WWW/ircdocs.html

This master site includes an IRC reference manual, IRC users' home page directory, logs from IRC chats, lists of chat channels with pages on the Web, and links to IRC lists, newsgroups, and resources online.

Directory of Writers' Workshops and Chats

The following organizations or writers' groups sponsor online chats and workshops. To find out more about each chat, and how to join, visit the companion Web sites. You will find detailed access information archived online at the Web sites.

@Writers
http://www.geocities.com/Athens/Acropolis/6608

@Writers Chat is sponsored by the "@Writers" newsletter team. Access can be had by using any IRC software and connecting to irc.prospero.com #Join channel

@Writers. Access instructions and chat times, topics, and schedules are posted at the Web site.

Friendly Pencil: Online Coaching for Writers
http://www.ilinks.net/~jkent/fp/

The Friendly Pencil supports a range of fee-based writing services and tutorials for new writers. Payment of an annual fee entitles subscribers to a range of tutorial and workshop learning options. Instruction is delivered via mailing lists, a private IRC channel, and e-mail.

The Green Room—Playwrights and Screenwriters Chat Room
http://www.teleport.com/~cdeemer/powwow.html

Charles Deemer, veteran playwright, hosts this private Web-based chat room for playwrights and screenwriters. For information on access—it's password protected—visit the Web site or e-mail Charles <cdeemer@teleport.com> for access information.

HTML (Hypertext Markup Language) Writers Guild Chat Channel
http://www.hwg.org/

The Writers Guild sponsors the #HWG chat channel for members to gather and discuss issues related to authoring and publishing in an HTML, Web-based environment. Access instructions are housed on the Web page under IRC Chat.

IRC Undernet Writers Page
http://www.getset.com/writers

This Web page introduces writers to the Undernet #writers channels and the many chats that occur there, generally weekly. Members' biographies, archives from past chats and workshops, writing resource links, subscription instructions to various writers' critique lists, and the e-mail newsletter "Writers Page" are featured. Undernet channels for writers are as follows: Writers Channel—#writers—a 24-hour channel on writing and the writer's life; Poetry Channel—#poetry—nightly readings by poets; Screenwriters Channel—#screenwriters—for screen- and scriptwriters; Teenwriters Channel—#youngwriters—for those 19 or younger; and Writers Cafe—#writerscafe—for socializing.

Mystery Place Chat—#Mystery
http://www.talkcity.com/mystery/

The Mystery Place, a general resource center for mystery writers and readers, sponsors live chats as well as live workshops on techniques and marketing tips from published mystery authors. Chats may be joined from the Web gateway if your browser supports Java, or from an IRC client.

Science Fiction & Fantasy Chats & Online Gaming
http://sflovers.rutgers.edu/Web/SFRG

For information on science fiction and fantasy chats and realms in the United Kingdom and the United States, check the Chat Channels and Role-Playing section of this master Science Fiction Resource Guide. Current projects include Hi-Fi Sci-Fi, a weekly #entertainment chat discussion room, and the David Brinn chat channel where participants role play in the Uplift Universe of writer David Brinn.

Screenwriters Online Chat
http://screenwriter.com/insider/ChatSOL.html

This page gives instructions on joining the regular chats on the screenwriters channel from Screenwriters Online. For those unfamiliar with IRC, instructions are posted on how to locate a client, and then how to download and install it.

SFF Net—Genre Writers Chats
http://www.sff.net/member/chat.htp

SFF Net—a private provider of online resources for writers in mystery, horror, sci-fi, and romance—sponsors Web-accessible chats. Anyone can browse chat rooms for free, but a monthly membership fee applies for regular access.

The Writer's BBS (Bulletin Board Service)
http://www.writersbbs.com

The Writer's BBS operates real-time chat forums. Their Web-based system requires some configuring and command knowledge similar to that used by IRC and other virtual chat formats. Information is provided in the Web Chat section on configuring for access to Writer's BBS synchronous talks.

Academic Writing Labs and Resources

Universities pioneered the use of the Internet for information sharing and networking. Small wonder, then, that teaching applications of the Net are being actively explored at academic centers. English, journalism, and communication departments are among the most active academic sectors pioneering new ways to tutor and teach in computer-mediated and networked environments.

If you teach writing on campus, or head an academic department that wants to transfer curriculum to a computer-mediated format or to a multiuser domain like a MUD, a MAUD, an IRC, or a MOO, make the National Writing Centers Association your first stop online. Among the helpful materials archived there is a directory to more than 170 academic Online Writing Labs (OWLs) and handouts on adopting curriculum and implementing teaching standards in cyberenvironments.

Diversity University uses the MOO environment to set up campus-like learning facilities where different virtual rooms serve different functions, like instruction and administration. Online users navigate through different rooms, undertaking different functions by typing lines of text commands. MOOs and MUDs require even more command knowledge to use than IRCs. To access them, you don't usually need separate software, but you must know how to telnet into a given online domain at a set time (See Chapter 16, "Finding and Retrieving Material on the Information Dirt Road: Telnet, FTP, Archie, Gopher, and Veronica," for information on Telnet).

For an interesting visit to an online writery in action, drop in at the University of Missouri Online Writery. Writing tutors there are employed to take writing questions via group e-mail (a mailing list) from University of Missouri students, but they will help others who need writing assistance. If you crave more immediate interaction, click-in at ZooMOO, a real-time multiuser chat room for writers of all kinds. If a MOO is new to you, primers and quick-tips are archived here to help you adopt an identity and log in as efficiently as possible.

If you're skeptical or just curious about how effective online or virtual instruction and tutoring can be, visit the Purdue University OWL and tap into its scholarly bibliography on OWLs. The bibliography chronicles leading research on pedagogical concerns.

Directory of Academic Resources on Computer-Mediated Communication

Alliance for Computers & Writing (ACW)
http://english.ttu.edu/acw/

The ACW is the premiere association for computer-mediated writing professionals. Archives include primers, a bank of course materials and handouts, and information on conferences and member activities. The Alliance also supports an active mailing list for instructors involved in computer-writing realms.

Composition Course Database
http://moo.du.org:8888/00anon/cybercomp

At this site, English instructors can search for academic course materials related to the teaching of writing and communications in cyberspace using Web, MOO, MUD, or IRC platforms.

DeVry Online Writing Support Center
http://www.devry-phx.edu/lrnresrc/dowsc

The DeVry center contains an impressive amount of information on composition in cyberspace and how to use digital dialogue tools. Instructors working online will find at the site a good one-stop primer on how to convert curriculum to electronic-delivery modes.

Diversity University—MOO
http://www.moo.du.org:8000/

This MOO-based instructional center provides a plethora of how-to manuals, instructional courses, and reference links to the use of Web and multiuser dialogue formats to instruct online in academic environments.

Internet Conversations
http://languagecenter.cla.umn.edu/lc/surfing/conversation

This is a great one-stop primer and resource archive from the University of Minnesota on IRC, MOO, MUD, MUSHes, and other multiuser conversational tools on the Net. The site includes a list of educational MOOs and teachers' tip sheets.

Journal of Computer-Mediated Communication (JCMC)
http://207.201.161.120/jcmc/index.html

JCMC, a joint project of the University of Southern California and the Hebrew University of Journalism, is a leading academic journal on legal, ethical, and social issues surrounding computer-mediated communications.

The Linguist List—MOO & MUD Sites
http://www.emich.edu/~linguist/moo.html

This site archives information, resources, primers, and links on the use of MOOs and MUDs in educational environments.

National Writing Centers Association (NWCA)—Writing Centers Online
http://www2.colgate.edu/diw/NWCA.html

The NWCA at Colgate University sponsors this master site to writing centers online, academic e-mail discussion groups, resources for academic writers, and informational brochures on tutoring in an online environment. Their directory of more than 170 academic OWLs, Web sites, and repositories is a must browse for faculty thinking of integrating the Net into writing or communication curriculum.

The Netoric Project
http://bsuuvc.bsu.edu/~00gisiering/netoric/netoric.html

Netoric is the Virtual Community for Scholars in Computers and Writing. The Project holds real-time chats and scholarly discussions online in a MOO environment every Tuesday evening at 8 P.M. with discussion times subject to change.

Online Resources for Writers
http://www.ume.maine.edu/~wcenter/resource.html

The University of Maine Writing Center maintains this resource directory to academic writing environments and computer-mediated communication journals and tools online.

Paradigm Online Writing Assistant
http://www.idbsu.edu/english/cguilfor/paradigm/

Chuck Guilford of the English Department at Boise State University maintains this online writers' handbook with tips on essay writing and editing in an online

HTML environment. The guide is used by Washington State University English teachers for teaching writing in an online environment.

Purdue Online Writing Lab (OWL)
http://owl.english.purdue.edu/

Purdue University maintains this model OWL site that allows browsers to peek into the action, access a scholarly annotated bibliography about online writing labs, retrieve teacher hand-outs, and follow links to a plethora of OWL-related sites of interest on the Web.

References for Writers
http://www.humberc.on.ca/~coleman/cw-ref.html

This is Chris Coleman's master Canadian directory of online style books, hypertext authoring projects, and hand-out repositories for use in academic writing instruction.

University of Illinois Writers' Workshop Handbook
http://www.english.uiuc.edu/cws/wworkshop/writer.html

This first-rate site includes a sample Writers' Handbook and a plethora of links to online resources for teachers of writing, literature, and English as a Second Language.

University of Missouri—Online Writery (OWL)
http://www.missouri.edu/~wleric/writery.html

Peek in here to see a model full-service academic writery in action. The Writery also sponsors the Writery-Cafe, a writers' discussion list. Browsers can register for the Writery-Cafe while at the Web site.

WriteMUX
http://www.visi.com/~ronda/writemux

WriteMUX is an educational multiuser domain. The WriteMUX archives a user's guide with detailed instructions on how to log on and navigate from room to room using a virtual multiuser interface. An Edguide details how academics can harness a multiuser environment to instruct in a group format.

CHAPTER 10

Searching for Advice and Camaraderie: *Usenet Newsgroups*

Usenet newsgroups started out in 1979, at Duke University, as an experiment by two students to see if they could get two mainframe computers to "talk" to each other. The experiment worked; the result, two decades later, is a formidable jungle of special discussion forums or electronic bulletin boards called newsgroups. An estimated 100,000 messages are posted daily to more than 22,000 newsgroups.

To begin, most newsgroups are not really newsy. Most are grassroots or industry-specific message boards where people with like interests congregate. Whatever your special interest, there is certain to be a newsgroup dedicated to the discussion of that interest. There is a newsgroup, for example, for people who simply want to whine about life (alt.life.sucks), and there is one for freelance journalists to discuss industry trends and exchange research tips (alt.journalism.freelance).

How Are They Organized?

Newsgroups are divided according to broad subject categories, called *computer hierarchies*. Following are the main hierarchies. Most services will carry these hierarchies for general browsing. New hierarchies are being added daily, however.

alt. = alternative

The alt. hierarchy broadly covers topics with alternative slants. The group alt.journalism.freelance, for example, is for freelance journalists looking to network and exchange research tips. The group alt.pagan is a discussion forum for those interested in pagan religions. The group alt.books.anne-rice allows fans and followers of vampire author Anne Rice to congregate and chat.

biz. = business

The biz. hierarchy supports forums that deal with commercial postings and transactions or sales, marketing, and advertising. Unlike other hierarchies, these exist for commercial purposes. The biz.books.technical group, for example, is a forum for the sale, barter, and commercial side of the technical books' trades. You'll find ads and "for sale" offers in any biz. hierarchy.

comp. = computers

The comp. hierarchy features forums dedicated to computer topics. The group comp.editors, for example, is a discussion forum on computerized text editors. The group comp.internet.library is a forum for issues related to electronic libraries.

misc. = miscellaneous

Discussions of everything under the sun and nothing in particular as it relates to one main topic are included in the catch-all misc. hierarchy. The group misc.writing, for example, is a high-volume group that attracts discussions on everything from how to syndicate your own newspaper column to how to query an agent.

news. = news

The news. hierachy is dedicated to news about the world of Usenet newsgroups. The group news.announce, for example, contains announcements about new Usenet newsgroups.

rec. = recreation

The rec. forums cover sports, leisure, recreation, and hobbies. For writers, many of the rec. groups are dedicated to the discussion of books by particular authors or other creative endeavors like recreational writing. The rec.arts.books.children group, for example, is a forum dedicated to the discussion of children's book. Post your own poems in rec.arts.poems or read the poetry posted there by others.

sci. = science and scientific research

The sci. hierarchy supports science discussions of all stripes, from astronomy to zoology. The forum sci.space.shuttle, for example, is a low-traffic group for the discussion of issues related to the space shuttle.

soc. = social issues and socializing

The soc. hierarchy supports forums for chatting and providing social support around personal issues like depression. The group soc.support.loneliness, for example, is a discussion forum for those dealing with loneliness. The group soc.culture.jewish is dedicated to a discussion of Jewish culture.

talk. = debate and talk forums

The talk. hierarchy supports forums on sometimes-controversial issues like euthanasia, women's rights, and atheism. The group talk.abortion, for example, is a forum on abortion rights.

Regional and Specialized Hierarchies

Depending on where you live, you may have access to a slew of specialized citywide, regional, or international newsgroups. Items for sale in Australia get posted to au.ads.forsale, for example. But if you live in Omaha, your local Internet provider may not subscribe to that particular newsgroup.

ClariNet is a special hierarchy issued from professional wire services. It is a feed for syndicated wire material, like Dave Barry's humor columns. You cannot post anything to ClariNet yourself. Unlike the other hierarchies, your service provider has to pay a subscription fee to carry ClariNet, and many do not carry it for this reason.

How Do Writers Use Newsgroups?

We've used newsgroups to locate people for human interest background on news stories, to search for freelance writing assignments, to network and socialize with other writers, to discuss topics like how much to charge for electronic book rights, and to keep up to date on innovations in areas that interest us. Because newsgroups bring together people with common interests, they can be great places to locate everyday folks who have a story to tell.

How to Access Newsgroups

Unlike mailing lists, which come to you via e-mail, you must go online to access newsgroups. Newsgroup messages are stored online. They are readable in bulletin-board style. Someone will post a message to a newsgroup the same way they would tack a message up on a public bulletin board. You go online, read the message, and reply to it or not as you wish. Messages on a common topic are called "threads." When you access a newsgroup, you can choose to read only one thread or all the threads in a newsgroup before logging off.

To access newsgroups you need two things. First, you need special software, called a *newsreader*. Second, you need an Internet connection that subscribes to the newsgroups for you, either a local Internet service provider (ISP) or a commercial access provider like America Online or CompuServe. Commercial services like America Online have "built in" newsreaders bundled with their own software. Alternatively, you can read and search newsgroups from the Web, at DejaNews or other sites.

How to Participate in Newsgroups

Most newsgroups are unmoderated. This means that anyone who has a thought can post it here publicly. Because most newsgroups are unmoderated, you may find a lot of messages like MAKE MILLIONS! and HOT! X-RATED! sprinkled inside them. Separating the wheat from the chaff can be tiresome but rewarding. Some newsgroups have literally been abandoned to spam advertisers, meaning that when you visit them they will look more like a poorly kept bulletin board in a seedy laundromat than an intellectual discussion forum on the advertised topic. You may have to be diligent in searching through newsgroups until you find the best ones for information or camaraderie.

If you're new to newsgroups and you want to learn more or practice reading and posting to newsgroups in a safe environment, visit the group news.newusers.questions. Feel free to post your help! questions here. You can also post simple "test messages" to see if you know what you're doing.

Some newsgroups receive so many postings that to keep up you will need to visit them every day or two. Other newsgroups see little traffic. You may find yourself the only one with a message to post to some groups, while you have to wade through thousands of inane messages to be heard on other groups.

Because most groups are unmoderated, they sometimes get overrun by small bands of people who fancy themselves experts on the topic at hand. For old-timers to insult those new to the group, or "newbies," is acceptable behavior in some of these groups. In general, you should mind your manners when participating in a newsgroup, just as you do when you participate in any public forum.

- Don't post in capital letters.

- Don't post blatantly commercial messages.

- Don't flame (insult) others in the group.

- Watch your language (what you write is being archived for posterity!).

- Do lurk and read messages for a few days before posting one of your own.

- Do read the FAQ file.

What's a FAQ File?

FAQ stands for *frequently asked questions*. Almost all newsgroups have FAQ files. These files have the answers to the most commonly asked questions by those new to the group. FAQ files are commonly posted once every week or month directly to the newsgroup so newbies can read them. Look for the FAQ file when you first join a newsgroup.

One word of caution about FAQs. Some provide a great introduction to the topic at hand, but others are poorly written, outdated, or authored by people whose opinions may be highly colored by their personal bias or commercial concerns. Read the FAQs but never assume that they are "the facts" in any objective sense of that word.

FAQ FTP archives
ftp: //rtfm.mit.edu/pub/usenet/news.answers

This ftp site archives all Usenet FAQs that have been posted to the newsgroup, news.answers. If you want to locate, download, and read the FAQ for any newsgroup before visiting or posting to that newsgroup, visit this site.

news.answers

This is a newsgroup full of FAQs on all imaginable topics.

How to Find and Search Newsgroups from the World Wide Web

Finding Newsgroups: Tile.Net/News
http://www.tile.net/news/

Tile.Net/News is the best search site on the Web if you're looking to locate all the newsgroups that discuss a particular topic. If you want to find all the "journalism" related newsgroups, for example, you can order a search on "journalism" and within seconds Tile.Net/News will give you a listing of all newsgroups dedicated to this topic.

Searching Newsgroups: DejaNews
http://www.dejanews.com

DejaNews is the best search engine on the Web for all newsgroups. Newsgroups stored on local servers archive messages only for an average of two weeks in order to conserve computer storage space. In contrast, DejaNews archives every message posted to the Usenet since March 1995.

To access DejaNews, you need to be able to access the Web. Once there, the DejaNews graphical interface allows you to input keyword searches. DejaNews will search more than 22,000 newsgroups simultaneously for any messages posted in the last year related to your keyword subject.

If you know someone who posts frequently to newsgroups on your topic, you can also execute a keyword search on their e-mail address and get, in return, a listing of all the postings they have made recently across newsgroups.

You can also post messages to multiple newsgroups from here. If you make multiple postings, do so with care. This practice, called "spamming," is frowned upon because it is commonly used by advertisers to post irrelevant ads to multiple newsgroups.

Directories of Writing-Related Newsgroups

The following is a selection of the most commonly visited writing-related newsgroups by topic area. New newsgroups spring up weekly and older ones may become inactive. Visit a master directory online, like Tile.Net, to search for new or additional newsgroups.

General Groups

alt.books.reviews (book reviews)

alt.usage.english (discussion of grammar, bibliographies, English usage)

misc.creativity (discussions on creativity of all forms)

misc.writing (issues related to writing and the writing life)

rec.arts.books (books and Internet book news)

rec.arts.books.marketplace (buying and selling books)

rec.arts.books.reviews (book reviews)

Journalism

alt.journalism (shop-talk for journalists and students)

alt.journalism.criticism (critical discussion of journalism)

alt.journalism.freelance (freelance writers)

alt.journalism.gay.press (gay or transgendered journalists and their colleagues)

alt.journalism.gonzo (Hunter Thompson's approach to journalism)

alt.journalism.gsn (journalism discussion)

alt.journalism.moderated (moderated discussion of the profession of journalism)

alt.journalism.music (music journalists)

alt.journalism.newspapers (newspaper journalists)

alt.journalism.objective (journalism discussion)

alt.journalism.photo (photojournalists)

alt.journalism.print (alternatives to print-based journalism)

alt.journalism.students (students of journalism)

Theme Groups

alt.books.technical (technical writing)

alt.books.purefiction (best-selling novels and how to write one)

misc.books.technical (technical writing and book news)

misc.writing.screenplays (writing and selling screenplays)

rec.arts.books.childrens (discussion of children's books)

rec.arts.books.hist-fiction (historical fiction)

rec.arts.int-fiction (interactive, gaming, or multimedia fiction)

rec.arts.movies.people (people in film and movies)

rec.arts.movies.production (discussion of filmmaking)

rec.arts.movies.reviews (movie reviews)

rec.arts.movies.tech (technical aspects of filmmaking)

rec.arts.mystery (mystery books)

rec.arts.poems (for the posting of poems)

rec.arts.prose (for the posting of prose)

rec.arts.sf.reviews (speculative and science fiction)

rec.arts.sf.written (speculative and science fiction written works)

rec.arts.theater (theater discussions)

rec.arts.theater.misc (theater discussions)

rec.arts.theater.musicals (musical theater discussions)

rec.arts.theater.plays (plays and play production issues)

rec.arts.theater.stagecraft (play production and technical issues)

Author-Specific Book Discussion Groups

The following groups are book, fan, and literary discussion groups dedicated to the works of the authors or literary movement (i.e., beat generation) in the newsgroup's title. Science fiction and speculative fiction authors tend to have the largest Net followings.

alt.books.anne-rice

alt.books.beatgeneration

alt.books.brian-lumley

alt.books.clive-barker

alt.books.crichton

alt.books.cs-lewis

alt.books.dean-koontz

alt.books.deryni

alt.books.h-g-wells

alt.books.isaac-asimov

alt.books.kurt-vonnegut

alt.books.m-lackey

alt.books.phil-k-dick

alt.books.sf.melanie-rawn

alt.books.stephen-king

alt.books.toffler

alt.books.tom-clancy

rec.arts.books.tolkien

rec.arts.sf.written.robert-jordan

rec.arts.startrek.reviews

Author-Specific Fan Clubs

The following groups are book and fan discussion groups dedicated to the work or spirit of the author or character in the newsgroup's title.

alt.fan.dave-barry

alt.fan.douglas-adams

alt.fan.dragonlance

alt.fan.dune

alt.fan.eddings

alt.fan.g-gordon-liddy

alt.fan.heinlein

alt.fan.hofstadter

alt.fan.holmes

alt.fan.james-bond

alt.fan.nathan.brazil

alt.fan.noam-chomsky

alt.fan.pern

alt.fan.piers-anthony

alt.fan.pratchett

alt.fan.robert-jordan

alt.fan.rumpole

alt.fan.rush-limbaugh

alt.fan.tolkien

alt.fan.tom-clancy

alt.fan.tom-peterson

alt.fan.tom-robbins

alt.fan.wodehouse

alt.fan.woody-allen

PART II

The Commercial Online Services

CHAPTER 11

Internet Service Providers vs. Commercial Online Services: *Punching Your Own Ticket to Ride*

Once upon a time, making a decision to "go online" from your home computer was fairly simple. You needed three basic things: your trusty home computer (if you were considering this online stuff, you had surely befriended that beast by now!); a device called a modem (short for *mod*ulate/*dem*odulate— what a modem actually does as it turns computer signals into phone signals and vice versa); and a phone jack with a live line behind it to accommodate your modem.

Once you were jacked-in, your only remaining decision was whether you'd go online with one of the large, smorgasbord commercial online services, like CompuServe or America Online, or choose to spend your time tooling around the smaller, home-grown world of bulletin board services, or BBS.

Bulletin boards still exist. They are primarily local or regional efforts. There are thousands upon thousands of them. For the most part, BBSs cater to local niche interests, such as computer gaming or programming. They also generally require some computer savvy to log onto and navigate. The BBS "back roads" are not for the faint of techno-heart. To explore the world of grassroots, homegrown bulletin boards, point your Web browser to the online home of *Boardwatch Magazine* <http://www.boardwatch.com>. *Boardwatch* is dedicated to following the BBS scene, and you'll find everything you need there if you want to test dial the scene.

The Rise of the Commercial Online Service

What has become much more popular in the last few years as a way of accessing the Internet are the national commercial online services—namely America Online and CompuServe. These services took the idea of a community bulletin board and meeting place and stretched it into a much larger vision of online life. These services built the first easy-to-access, and navigate, large online neighborhoods. You can dial into these neighborhoods from any point in the United States. They provide meeting boards, informational libraries, shopping services, and chat rooms dedicated to hundreds upon hundreds of topics and interest groups, rather than single niche interests.

National commercial services like America Online are designed to turn cyber-cruising into a leisure activity that requires as little knowledge of computer command log-on lingo as possible. Upon registering with one of these packaged services, you'll receive a diskette or two in the mail with the appropriate start-up directions. A combination of monthly and hourly fees gives you point-and-click access to the otherwise private online neighborhoods that have been created in the name of the first national dial-up services—services like America Online, CompuServe, Microsoft Network, Delphi, and Prodigy.

National online service or BBS: these were the original two on-ramps to online life. Both initially limited your cyber-travels to the domain you had jacked into. If you connected to America Online, you could roam America Online far and wide, but you could never venture beyond its borders. You could access only what America Online had housed on its main computer banks in Vienna, Virginia, for its members to access. Similarly, if you dialed into your local community bulletin board, local community chat was all you'd get.

These days, things are more complicated because it is now possible to log onto the Internet at large using a commercial service like CompuServe and

America Online. Once logged onto CompuServe, for example, you can now either roam around inside CompuServe—exploring their proprietary content as you'd explore the inside of one very large informational mall—or you can choose to leave CompuServe. You can choose to point-and-click your way out of CompuServe's main computers in Columbus, Ohio, onto the Internet at large.

The Internet is nothing more than a series of computers all over the world that are equipped to dial into each other. The Internet serves as a vast superhighway, connecting once-separate worlds to each other, and to a whole lot more. A superhighway without a good vehicle, however, is just one wicked, unpaved road. Selecting the appropriate Internet service provider (ISP) or vehicle for getting onto the Net is like finding the right set of wheels in which to cruise the world.

Think there are a lot of cars to choose from? Right now, in addition to national commercial services like America Online and CompuServe, there are more than 3,000 free-standing ISPs ready and willing to punch your "ticket to ride"—to become your online entrance ramp.

Commercial Online Service or ISP?

Should you go with an Internet service provider (ISP) or a commercial on-line service to get onto the Internet? ISPs are newer creatures that rose to prominence primarily as cheap toll roads onto the Information Super-highway. Whereas America Online and CompuServe were charging $2.95 per hour for log-on time, independent ISPs came along and began charging a flat rate of $19.95 per month for unlimited online time. So if you wanted cheap Internet access, you went with an ISP. If you preferred to have all your information within easy reach and needed a bit of technological hand-holding, you paid the premium per hour price for a commercial online service like America Online.

It's not that simple anymore. These days, for the same amount of money as an ISP, online services give you a consistent interface, easy access and interesting content, and a sense of community that, according to some, is less likely to be found on the Web.

The decision as to which way you go these days to get on the Net depends on how you prefer to travel. If you're a world traveler who likes to book tour packages, with every detail of the travel itinerary mapped out for you, then a packaged commercial service like America Online would probably suit you best. On the other hand, if you're the type who likes to throw a change of clothes and a few Berlitz guides into a backpack and book a transatlantic flight on a whim, you might be happier with a simple ISP account.

One big advantage to the commercial services is that they provide content that only their subscribers can access. America Online, for example, sponsors a treasure chest of online chats, workshops, and tutorials through their Writers Club. You can't fully access the AOL Writers Club unless you subscribe to America Online. The same is true of CompuServe. Inside CompuServe, you'll find rich fields of information and professional networking forums that are worked by some of America's leading journalists. You can't get to most of these forums or databases unless you are a CompuServe subscriber.

Subscribing to a Provider: You Better Shop Around

Local or National ISP?

Many Internet veterans prefer local ISPs to the larger national providers. Local ISPs are more likely to offer training to their subscribers and sport rates equal to or slightly lower than those of the nationals. The smaller subscription base of a local ISP can mean less competition for open dial-in lines, so some local providers may have better performance and more reliable connections.

But the performance records of local Internet services can run the gamut from stellar to dismal—that's why you should always ask about other subscribers' experiences before you take the plunge. As is true in many venues, word of mouth is worth its weight in gold.

Is That a Local Call?

First and foremost, make *sure* that your telephone access will be a local call. If a provider does not offer a local access number in your neck of the woods, no matter how attractive their package sounds, keep looking! Nothing can darken your view of the online world as quickly as several hundred dollars in unexpected long distance phone charges! While we like both America Online and

CompuServe, for different reasons, as they have different content for writers, we have remained with our account with America Online because we live in a rural area where America Online has a local access dial-in. When we call into CompuServe, on the other hand, we must dial and pay long-distance charges.

If you are likely to travel with a laptop computer and want access from various locations, the large national providers (both the ISPs and the online services) are more likely to have local access numbers in major cities.

A top-notch starting point for shopping for a local ISP, if you can gain access to a Web browser for a quick ride, is "The List" at <http://thelist.iworld.com>. Searchable by country, state, area code, or domain name, the entries here include hotlinks to ISPs' Web pages nationwide.

How Much Time Do You Need?

Next, get a sense, if you can, of how much time you spend online and compare charges based on that. If you're going online strictly to send and retrieve e-mail, you'll probably be spending no more than five hours a month online. If you happen to be an AT&T long-distance customer, AT&T offers five free hours per month for your first year of access. If you prefer the style and content of an online service, $9.95 buys you five hours of access per month on America Online, CompuServe, or Prodigy.

If you spend more than eight hours per month online, you should consider an unlimited access plan. America Online, Microsoft Network, and Prodigy (as well as some other national ISPs such as SpryNet and PSINet, and many local providers) all offer a monthly flat rate of $19.95 for unlimited time.

Service, Please

Be sure your ISP support team doesn't work bankers' hours. Telephone technical support should be available 24 hours a day, seven days a week, a toll-free call away. The claim of free support is not enough—even toll-free support is no bargain if you constantly reach voice mail and get no callbacks! Once again, word-of-mouth recommendations might prove important.

If you want to set up your own Web page, most ISPs will give you the server space to do so, but only a few will provide training or support in this area. This is an area where, thanks to proximity and fewer customers, local providers have an edge. ISPs offer from one megabyte to an unlimited amount of space for personal Web pages, and prices vary, so shop carefully if this is a priority. Both America Online and CompuServe provide their own online support and packaged online tutorials that make creating your own Web page off their main service tree fairly easy.

What's the Speed Limit?

Virtually every provider enables you to connect at 28.8 kbps, the minimum recommended modem speed for Internet travel. Installed phone lines in some rural areas may prevent a 28.8 connection, but that is changing as the country becomes increasingly wired. The majority of Internet users are connecting with 28.8-kbps modems, but that doesn't mean you get equal performance from all services with a bank of 28.8-kbps modems. Traffic makes the difference.

The Big Four commercial online services (America Online, CompuServe, Microsoft Network, and Prodigy) have millions of subscribers who suck up bandwidth as they load fancy artwork and access services. Many users report that during peak periods they are able to get only a slow connection, if any at all. America Online became infamous in 1996–1997 for not having enough modems and support services to support the number of members it had recruited. Some people spent hours just trying to log onto AOL during peak hours.

On the other hand, even small local providers have traffic problems if they lack sufficient hardware to handle the peak volume of calls. You may have a fast connection, but nothing is slower than a busy signal. How often you get busy signals will depend on your provider's customer-to-modem ratio, which should be between 8-to-1 and 12-to-1. You may not be told an accurate customer-to-modem ratio if you ask the service provider—they want to sell you on their service! As customer ranks swell, some providers (even the big ones!) have trouble keeping pace with hardware upgrades.

Packing a Cybersuitcase

Choosing a provider is the first step. If you do not go with a packaged commercial service like America Online or CompuServe, you will need software for each of the popular Internet activities. With the commercial services, you get one integrated software application that gives you easy point-and-click access to all cyber-cruising activities.

Free-standing ISPs are more confusing to deal with, especially for newbies. ISPs generally offer separate versions of e-mail clients, Web browsers, newsgroup readers, and other software. Some will supply licensed copies of these programs on a set of diskettes or a CD-ROM. Some might have you download shareware versions of various software tools from their server—a process that may be outside your comfort zone if you are not very technologically inclined.

A tremendous advantage to using commercial services like America Online or CompuServe is that they will provide you with one piece of integrated software that will give you access to all online and Internet access functions. If you're a computer or Internet newbie, the no-brainer one-piece of software approach offered by a commercial online service will definitely ease your travels.

Exploring the Commercial Online Services

The next two chapters give you a detailed peek inside America Online and CompuServe—the special services and content they offer their subscribers, with a particular eye toward what they offer writers. These two commercial services are reviewed in depth because they are the largest online services, and they offer both quality internal content and easy Internet access.

If you're interested in looking at the other major commercial services, you can visit their sites on the Web or call their toll-free numbers to get a free starter kit. Microsoft is the newer of the two and will run only a Windows platform. Prodigy is the older of the two and still offers a variety of internal services for fiction and genre writers in particular—though it has been troubled by a steadily declining membership base over the last few years.

Prodigy
800-PRODIGY
http://www.prodigy.com

Microsoft Network
800-426-9400
http://www.msn.com

America Online: *A Haven for Fiction Writers*

America Online
8619 Westwood Center
Vienna, Virginia 22182-2285
703-448-8700
800-827-6364
http://www.aol.com/

Cost: $19.95 per month for unlimited use. Limited-use payment plans are also available. A free 30-day trial membership is available. Fees are subject to change.

Early online services required users to fumble through computer command lingo to log on and navigate. By pioneering a pictorial point-and-click interface, and by implementing an aggressive marketing campaign, America Online (AOL) became the online service of choice for the technologically challenged. AOL is America's largest commercial online service, supporting a membership of more than 8 million subscribers.

You move through AOL by clicking on pictures (called icons) or by using drop-down menus. The point-and-click navigation system that proved to be

AOL's electronic trump card in the online business is constantly undergoing revisions to make access faster and friendlier for users.

AOL's strength lies in the breadth of the content it provides to subscribers. Over the years, AOL members have built strong internal clubs or forums where like-minded people can congregate to exchange tips and ideas, chat in real-time rooms, and network. Writers, especially fiction and genre writers, have been quick to join AOL—and once there, reluctant to leave. The Writers Club (Keyword: **Writers**) is the primary place on AOL where authors gather for information, mentoring, and networking.

Overview

When you sign onto AOL, a main menu pops up on your screen. This menu lists more than 20 separate areas or "channels" of developed information and services that are available only to AOL members. Channels, which may change from time to time as the system reorganizes, include: Computers & Software, Digital City, Entertainment, Games, Health & Fitness, The Hub, International, Internet Connection, Kids Only, Learning & Culture, Life, Styles & Interests, Marketplace, Music Space, Newsstand, People Connection, Personal Finance, Reference, Sports, Style, Today's News, and Travel.

To explore a particular channel once you are logged onto AOL, simply click on that channel's graphical headline or banner. To move deeper into any one channel, keep clicking on the icons. New levels of information will pop up until you have exhausted what any one channel has to offer.

The first thing you'll want to learn to use on AOL is the keyword system, because once you're logged onto AOL, keywords allow you to bypass the screen layers you would otherwise have to click through to get to your final destination. Inputting keywords to jump around on AOL will allow you to be more targeted in your online use.

Each main area of AOL has a keyword associated with it. If you want to go directly to the Writers Club (located inside the Life, Styles & Interests Channel), press your Control key and the letter "K." A keyword dialogue box will pop up on your screen asking you to type in the keyword for the area you want to visit. Type in "writers," press your Return key, and you will be transported to the Writers Club main menu. You can access a complete directory of navigational keywords by going to the keyword "Keyword." Keywords, by the way, are *not* case sensitive. You can input WRITERS or writers as a keyword on AOL.

A complete review of all the resources housed within AOL would be encyclopedic in length. In this chapter, we purposefully limit our review of AOL to destinations that contain the best writing and book-related content. Once logged onto AOL, you will discover a vast mall of informational resources and entertainment possibilities coming from the more than 20 channels that AOL makes available to its members. The Travel Channel, for example, though not covered in this chapter, contains travel tips, airline and travel booking bureaus, travel-related stores, and still more that are related to recreational and business travel needs.

Life, Styles & Interests Channel

The Life, Styles & Interests channel hosts an exciting mix of special-interest associations. If you need to locate people to interview for a feature story, this section is well worth a visit. If you were writing a story on seniors in cyberspace, for example, you would find people to interview and first-rate background material in the forums maintained by SeniorNet and the American Association of Retired People (AARP).

The Writers Club (Keyword: **Writers**)

If you're in the business of writing, AOL's Writers Club is the place to be, especially if you're a fiction writer. Input the keyword "writers" and you'll be transported to the Writers Club main menu. From the main menu, you can select from the following Writers Club activities or from other feature events.

Writers Chat (Keyword: **Wcchat**)

A monthly calendar is maintained of free online chats, workshops, and discussion groups. Topics include most fiction markets, as well as some on the business of writing. Dark fiction and horror, mystery, suspense, romance, science fiction, children's writing, starting and running your own press, finding an agent, writing basics, novel writing, Christian magazine writing, screenwriting, and poetry are common topics. More than 40 regular real-time chats occur each month. Both Romance Writers (Keyword: **Wcrg**) and Teen Writers (Keyword: **Teenwriters**) maintain their own chat areas on AOL.

Writers Cafe (Keyword: **Writers**)

The Cafe is a 24-hour chat room where you can drop-in on a whim for live, real-time conversation with fellow writers. The chat here is free-form and generally quite friendly. Join a topic in progress or rant and rave about your own current creative endeavors. Input Keyword: **Writers**, then select "chat" from the main menu.

Mentor Program (Keyword: **Writers**)

Mentoring can be an important part of learning any new craft. In this area, AOL lists the biographies of members who have volunteered to mentor others online. Mentors are available in nonfiction; technical and business; horror, fantasy, and science fiction; romance; poetry; song writing; screenwriting and playwriting; children and young adult; journalism; mystery and suspense; and specialty nonfiction. Journalism and nonfiction are less well represented, however. Input Keyword: **Writers**, then select "mentor program" from the main menu.

Message Boards (Keyword: **Writers**)

The Message Boards are veritable treasure chests of information and networking connections for writers. Visit the boards to get the opinions of your peers on the best software for handling scriptwriting or to scout for freelance job opportunities. Input Keyword: **Writers**, then select "Messages" from the main menu. Categories to read from or post to include conferences and workshops, copywriting, children's writers, comedy/humor writing, journalism/newswriting, nonfiction writing, playwriting and theater, readers and reading, science fiction/fantasy, horror, mystery fiction, writers markets, writers unions and groups, technical writing, screenwriting, poetry, and editing/indexing/translating.

The Business of Writing (Keyword: **Writers**)

This helpful section includes tips on writing and promoting your work as well as an advice column from Lary Crews, a freelance writer and writing instructor for AOL. The Non-Fiction FAQs or frequently asked question file authored by Stephen Morrill is a very helpful introduction to common questions that beginners ask about writing for money. The *New Writers Market News*, archived online, features magazines and periodicals that solicit work from freelance writers. Input Keyword: **Writers**, then select "The business of writing" from the main menu.

The Learning & Culture Channel

Books & Writing (Keyword: Books)

Barron's BookNotes (Keyword: **Barron's**)

Can't remember the name of that rooster in the *Canterbury Tales?* Search or download Barron's *BookNotes* online. Consult these detailed plot and character summaries to help you along.

Book Central—Cafe Books (Keyword: **Cafe Books**)

Book Central houses message forums for book reading groups. Join in on more than 90 book reading groups to discuss works as diverse as those by Jane Austen or Stephen King.

The Book Report (Keyword: **Book Report**)

Visit the Book Report to chat in the message forums with Men Who Love Books or to chat about Books I Hid from My Parents. A Personals section allows you to connect with other single, literate souls nationwide.

Fictional Realm (Keyword: **Fictional Realm**)

The Fictional Realm supports online chats, message forums, features, and archives in the areas of science fiction, horror, fantasy, romance, screenwriting, TV writing, comics, and interactive (computer game) fiction.

Just Reviews (Keyword: **Books**)

Book reviews are archived from the *Critics Choice*, *Entertainment Weekly*, and Moms Online.

Oprah's Book Club (Keyword: **Oprah**)

Reviews, chats, and discussion forums organized around the books that talk-show host Oprah Winfrey recommends to her national viewing audience.

Online Campus (Keyword: Courses)

Online Courses (Keyword: **Courses**)

AOL's online campus offers writers two opportunities: the first is the chance to take an online course in a new genre—there are courses in areas such as travel writing and romance novel writing; the second is to teach a course for self-promotional reasons or for profit. When a course is first offered, anyone may register for free. Instructors also agree to teach the course for free for the first session. If a course runs for subsequent sessions, a fee of from $25 to $50 is charged. Instructors retain a small percentage of the fees collected by AOL.

University of California Extension (Keyword: **UCX**)

The Center for Media & Independent Learning (CMIL) of the University of California offers an array of online courses. Courses of interest to writers include undergraduate degree-credit courses in short story writing, technical writing, and popular fiction.

The Arts

Afterwards Cafe (Keyword: **Afterwards**)

The Afterwards Cafe is a central meeting place for the culturally inclined. The Zeitgeist message boards cover theater, art education, music, books, literature, the business of books, Internet sites for artists, Broadway, film, artists' grants, the nature of art, classical music, opera, and evolving issues about arts and humanities online. The Afterwards Cafe Library Archive contains articles, poems, and works in progress from AOL members. Upload your own original works or download the works of others.

Newsstand Channel

AOL showcases the electronic editions of more than 100 periodicals. Back issues of many of these magazines and periodicals are archived online for free downloading. This can make your research much easier. Searching magazine archives is a great way to spark new story ideas or to get a feel for a magazine before you formulate a freelance query. If you're interested in the future of electronic publishing, AOL is a good place to explore what's happening as magazines go online and interactive. Many magazines offer enriched interactive editions online.

The *New York Times* hosts "@Times," an electronic edition and archive service on AOL. The "Books of the Times" section inside the "Arts & Entertainment

Guide" features book reviews, annual pieces on books and publishing, best-sellers' lists, a live weekly book chat, and message boards for discussing the literary life.

Today's News Channel

Late-breaking world and regional news from Reuters Hourly News Summary service is archived inside this channel. News areas include sports, politics, lifestyle, business, and weather. Read only the highlights, or access the news in depth. Once you're online, a search feature lets you locate archived summaries and press releases from the Associated Press (AP), Business Wire (BSW), PR Newswire, and Sports Ticker (STK).

News Desktop Delivery (Keyword: NewsProfiles)

Too busy to go online and hunt and peck through cyberspace for your daily news fix? Sign up to have customized news delivered via e-mail to your desktop on a daily basis. Specify the topics that interest you, and AOL's news service will automatically select, bundle, and e-mail news to you on your specified topic areas.

Reference Channel

Need a quick electronic fact check on the number of active volcanoes in the Western world? The Reference Channel supports several internal reference materials and provides gateways out of AOL into reference works stored on the Web.

Dictionaries (Keyword: **Dictionaries**)

Merriam-Webster's Collegiate, Kids, and *Medical* dictionaries are stored online. *The Dictionary of Cultural Literacy* and *Wall Street Words* are also available.

Encyclopedias (Keyword: **Encyclopedia**)

Compton's Living Encyclopedia, The Columbia Concise Encyclopedia, and *Grolier's Multimedia Encyclopedia* are searchable on AOL.

Quotations (Keyword: **Quotation**)

Can't remember who said what this century? Search the *New York Public Library's 20th Century Quotations*.

Bookstores

Barnes & Noble (Keyword: **Barnes**)

Barnes & Noble, America's largest book retailer, supports an online catalog of more than 1 million titles, with 30 percent off hardcovers and 20 percent off paperbacks.

Lamba Rising (Keyword: **Lamba Rising**)

One of America's leading distributors of gay and lesbian books, music, and videos, Lamba Rising supports an online catalog as well as gay and lesbian book discussion groups.

Read USA Online Bookstore (Keyword: **Read USA**)

Read USA allows browsers to order titles online. The associated Book Nook provides a chat space for author interviews and special monthly book events.

Writers Club Store (Keyword: **WC Store**)

The Writers Club maintains an online bookstore that features the best titles in writers' reference books, the business of writing, and genre writing. The store also carries writers' software, T-shirts, and other items.

Internet Connection Channel

Inside the Internet Connection Channel you'll find all the information and tools needed to get started exploring features housed on the Internet outside AOL, like the World Wide Web and Gopherspace. The Internet Connection Channel offers an impressive array of easy-to-understand primers and FAQ files on common Internet tools and procedures, like FTP (File Transfer Protocol) and WAIS (Wide Area Information Search). The tools provided on the Internet Channel make Internet access as easy as it can get. If you're new to the Internet, AOL provides an intuitive newsgroup reader, as well as a fairly intuitive Web browsing system.

If you've not a clue what the Internet is, or how to access its many informational treasures from AOL, input keyword "Net Help" and you'll land in the Internet help station on AOL where you can read about Net tools or post a distress message for AOL's Answer Man.

Many of AOL's internal channels are adding clickable gateway links out of AOL, onto the specialized resources of the Internet at large. For example, the Reference Channel is currently being beefed up with clickable links to reference sites that exist on the Web, like the Modern Language Association's style guide Web site. The Writers Club now houses a Web section that lists sites of interest to writers on the Web, like Bookwire, a super site of book-related sites on the Internet.

One caveat: when traffic is heavy on AOL, the task of getting out of the AOL system and onto the Internet at large can range in difficulty from daunting to impossible. Though Internet access is never a sure thing, when you access the Net from an internal system like AOL be prepared to face heightened internal system problems like slow-downs caused by heavy prime time usage.

Unfortunately, since the fall of 1996, when AOL began offering unlimited time online for a flat monthly rate, the service has been difficult to log onto in some urban areas. Access during the evening peak hours has been especially difficult for some members. New modem lines are being added to ease the access problem as this book goes to print. Subscribers who live in rural areas may not be able to access the service without incurring long distance dial-in charges. Before committing to a long-term subscription, we recommend you take the free 30-day trial membership to test your access ability.

CompuServe: *The Electronic Press Room*

CompuServe
5000 Arlington Centre Boulevard
P. O. Box 20212
Columbus, Ohio 43220
814-457-8600
800-524-3388
http://www.compuserve.com

Cost: $9.95 per month for five hours of online time with $2.95 for each additional hour. $24.95 per month for Super Value plan of 20 hours of usage. Premium database services are charged at additional rates. A free 30-day trial membership is available. Rates are subject to change.

CompuServe is a pioneer in the online information game. Though its membership is smaller than America Online's, it tends to be frequented by a more professional news- and business-oriented clientele. CompuServe has built a solid reputation as "the" online service for heavy-duty news hounds. That reputation is well-deserved. If you're the Clark Kent type, or if you write for technology, medical, legal, or the business/finance beats, you'll probably enjoy pounding CompuServe's electronic pavement. The JForum, or Journalism

Forum, in CompuServe was founded in 1985, and it remains to this day a first-class electronic press club, supporting innovative professional discussion and debate forums.

The wealth of specialized news and knowledge databases stored inside CompuServe makes its nearest commercial online competitor, America Online, appear electronically feeble-minded. CompuServe serves as an electronic gateway to hundreds of high-quality business and professional research services like Dialog, TRW, and Dun & Bradstreet, through IQuest (GO: **IQUEST**). For international news and information, CompuServe remains peerless. *Der Spiegel* (the German equivalent to *Time* magazine), the *Jerusalem Post*, and the *London Theatre Reviews* represent just a few of the international media outlets that are archived inside CompuServe.

On the downside, CompuServe's competitive edge may be a precarious perch. While journalists continue to gather on CompuServe, making it the indisputable electronic press club of the online world, many competitive subscription-based databases like EyeQ, Lexis-Nexis, and NewsPage, are setting up independent shop on the Internet at large.

Most premium database and news services operating within CompuServe charge on a pay-per-view scheme, making them expensive to access. (These services are clearly identified with a $ sign once you log onto CompuServe.) If you have to pay hourly online charges (billed to you by CompuServe) *plus* a per-article fee directly to the database that you are accessing, research can become an expensive adventure.

The idea of accessing the richly stuffed Business Database Plus service, located within CompuServe's Reference section, may make the newshound in you howl in delight. But paying the additional $15 per hour and $1.50 per article to access this database might also make you growl in financial despair—unless you happen to be a writer with a hefty corporate expense account.

Once you're logged on with CompuServe, click the GO button and type in "rates" to arrive at the online center which details CompuServe's rates on premium news services.

Navigating

When you log onto CompuServe, a main screen pops up with about 16 categories of service identified. (This graphical interface may vary with the version of the software you run, but the services will remain the same.) You can point-and-click your way into News & Weather, Computing, Games, Health, Home & Living, Internet, Sports, Professions, Recreation & Hobbies, Business, Finance, Home & Leisure, Arts & Entertainment, Search, Travel, or Shopping. As with all online services, categories may be added or deleted as the service evolves. The News & Weather (news search), Arts & Culture (books), and Profession areas (media, journalism, and publishing) will command the lion's share of cybertime for most writers.

The New Member Welcome Center is a good place to cut your electronic teeth. To arrive there, click on the GO button (it looks like a green GO traffic light) on the top of your screen bar. Type in the word "welcome." The system will boot you into the Welcome Center. Once logged onto CompuServe, you can jump directly to specific areas by using GO words.

You can use the Find feature to explore CompuServe's niches in subjects of interest to you—like "writer" and "books." Like Keywords on America Online, the Find feature on CompuServe is a great navigational tool for getting around online in the most expedient manner. To arrive at the Find/Search center from anywhere within CompuServe, click the GO button and type in "Find."

A complete review of all the resources housed within CompuServe would be encyclopedic in length. In this chapter, we purposefully limit our review of CompuServe to destinations that contain the best writing, research, and book-related content. Once logged onto CompuServe, you will discover a vast mall of informational resources and entertainment possibilities coming from 16 or more separate content areas. Begin your exploration of CompuServe with the following writing hot spots profiled, then branch out to CompuServe's other areas, such as Sports and Entertainment, to fully sample all that CompuServe has to offer.

Professional Forums

You can use CompuServe's blue-ribbon Professional Forums to gather background data for your writing, arrange interviews with industry experts, search for freelance writing assignments, or network with like-minded souls. CompuServe supports more than 2,000 forums. To locate a forum, click on the Find button on your Compuserve screen. Select the "Search by Subject" option and type in the kind of forum you seek—for example "journalism" or "writer" or "news" or "book." The system will automatically kick up a menu of sites related to your keyword. The menu will also list the GO word for each forum or area.

All forums have three sections: message boards (post a query for other professionals); library files (retrieve or upload articles and special reports); and conference rooms (for group lectures, workshops, and special gatherings). Professional Forums are the richest, most exciting part of the CompuServe experience. Compared to America Online, CompuServe sustains more professional forums in commercial writing and journalism, while simultaneously being less rich in resources, workshops, and gatherings for fiction genre writers. We chronicle the following forums most frequented by writers.

Book Preview Forum (GO: **PREVIEW**)

Located in Arts & Entertainment, the Preview Forum sponsors guest appearances by authors, electronic book signings, and author interviews. The library houses archives of online sessions by prior guest authors. The archive is divided into sub-areas of literature and can be searched by genre—romance, poetry, mystery— or by subject category.

Broadcast Professionals Forum (GO: **BPForum**)

Professionals in radio, TV, and audio media and broadcasting gather here to discuss programming, network technologies, emerging trends, and FCC policies.

Desktop Publishing Forum (GO: **DTPFORUM**)

This forum is a center for those involved in desktop and electronic publishing for fun or profit. Design, writing, production, printing, and marketing strategies are discussed.

Electronic Word Forum (GO: **EWORD**)

EWORD is a gathering place for those involved in electronic and online publishing, including audio, Web publishing, multimedia authoring, gaming, CD-ROM, and software development.

Internet Publishing Forum (GO: **INETPUB**)

This special forum is dedicated to a discussion of issues related to publishing and marketing on the World Wide Web and in the interactive multimedia realm.

Journalism Forum (GO: **JFORUM**)

JFORM, founded in 1985 as one of the first CompuServe Forums, welcomes new and seasoned journalists in all beats. Areas are maintained for freelancers, new media workers, print reporters, broadcast and photojournalists, and those interested in computer-assisted and Internet reporting. A members-only, press-club-type area is maintained for members of the NASW, ASJA, and APMTC. The JFORUM also maintains pages on the Web <http://www.jforum.org>.

Literary Forum (GO: **LITFORUM**)

Located in Arts & Entertainment, the Literary Forum supports the discussion of books, authors, and ideas. Recreational and academic readers are welcome.

PR & Marketing Forum (GO: **PRSIG**)

Public relations and marketing professionals gather here to network and learn more about the craft by sifting through the vast how-to industry-oriented library archives and specialized databases.

Professional Publishing Forum ($) (GO: **PROPUB**)

The Pro Publishing Club charges a small membership fee of $3 per month for access. The Forum serves those with a commercial interest in the publishing industry, including those in print, electronic, and other specialized areas.

Romance Forum (GO: **ROMANCE**)

Located in Arts & Entertainment, the Romance Forum is a general area for writers and readers of Romance literature. (A sign-on dialog box cautions browsers that this is not a Forum for those interested in the personal aspects of romance—for example, dating.)

SF Literature Forum 2 (GO: **SFLITTWO**)

Located in Arts & Entertainment, this Forum is for news, views, and book reviews of science fiction, fantasy, and horror works. There is also a companion SF/Fantasy Literature Forum (GO: **SFLIT**) in Arts & Entertainment.

TW Authors Forum (GO: **TWAUTHORS**)

The Authors Forum welcomes accomplished and beginning wordsmiths. The Forum offers special conferences and workshops in science fiction, poetry, children's writing, and crime and mystery. Marketing and publishing information is archived in the library section.

Working from Home Forum—Writers & Editors Section (GO: **WORK**)

The Working from Home Forum is designed for any type of home-based business owner or telecommuters. Writers and editors, who often work from home, have their own section where issues related to publishing and freelancing get hashed out.

News & Weather

The news and reference section of CompuServe contains more than 130 separate services. Some are pay-per-view premium services, and some are free magazines like *Money* and *People*. Free wire and late-breaking news services include Business Wire, Reuters, and the CNN Forum.

Pay-per-view or download areas are identified with a ($) on CompuServe menus. To find out about premium services and billing rates, input the GO word RATES when online. CompuServe is especially rich in pay-per-view international and global news services as well as business and finance, and health. Following are selected news services.

Business Wire (GO: **BIZWIRE**)

This free area archives news and press releases from Business Wire, the wire service dedicated to business, finance, and corporate news.

Executive News Service ($) (GO: **ENS**)

A customizable search and clipping service that gathers the news continuously for you from major wire services like Dow Jones, Reuters, UPI, AP Financial, AP U.S. & World, AP Sports, and the *Washington Post*. The news is then stored online in electronic folders for you to read when you are ready. The cost is $15 per hour for the time spent logged onto the service area.

Newspaper Archives ($) (GO: **NEWSARCHIVE**)

DIALOG Information Services operates this full-text retrieval archive of 55 papers in the United States and the United Kingdom. Regional papers, like the *Akron Beacon Journal*, *The Atlanta Constitution*, and *The Houston Post* are featured. Costs vary by publication but begin at $1 per article.

New York Newslink Forum (GO: **NEWYORK**)

New York Newslink is sponsored by Gannett Suburban Newspapers. The Forum welcomes New Yorkers, ex–New Yorkers, and those headed to the Big Apple area for business or pleasure.

UK Newspaper Library ($) (GO: **UKPAPERS**)

Leading European and United Kingdom papers are archived online here through an arrangement with N2K Telebase information services. The *Daily & Sunday Telegraph, Financial Times, Guardian, Herald,* and *Tass* are some of the papers with full-text retrieval options. Full-text retrieval rates begin at $1 per article and vary by publication.

Research—IQuest InfoCenter (GO: **IQUEST**)

IQuest, a service of Telebase Systems, offers centralized access to services from Dialog, NewsNet, Data-Star, CD Plus, and other information retrieval companies. Following are some of the more popular IQuest databases, each charging for search and retrieval services. Scanning and retrieval rates start at $1 and end at $42 per article for express delivery options.

Ziff-Davis, the publishing giant, operates several Database Plus services, including Business Database Plus and Computer Database Plus. Article access fees range from 25¢ to several dollars per download.

Business Database Plus ($) (GO: **BUSDB**)

A searchable database that houses hundreds of specialized reports, journals, newsletters, and full-text business articles. The charge is 25¢ per minute, plus $1.50 per article download.

Computer Database Plus ($) (GO: **COMPDP**)

A searchable database that archives the articles and abstracts from trade, popular, and professional computer and technology magazines like *PC Week, InfoWorld,* and *MacWeek.* Charges begin at 25¢ per minute with a $1 per article download.

Health Database Plus ($) (GO: **HLTDB**)

A health, wellness, and medical knowledge archive that pulls material from more than 50 journals, newsletters, company wellness pamphlets, and magazines like *American Health, Morbidity and Mortality Weekly, The New England Journal of Medicine,* and *Sportsmedicine.* Charges start at $1 per article.

Knowledge Index ($) (GO: **KI**)

Knowledge Index, a service of Dialog, is a popular mega-search package that gives researchers access to 100 full-text databases in 26 subject areas on a variety of general, professional, and subject areas. More than 50,000 journals are accessible through this bundled all-in-one research service. Journals are as specialized as those in law (720 law journals) and engineering. Subject databases cover everything from agriculture to education (ERIC) to the Philosopher's Index. Newspapers and professional report media are also included in the one-shot search service. A $21 per hour surcharge applies.

Magazine Database Plus ($) (GO: **MAGDB**)

Magazine Database Plus is a Ziff-Davis gateway into 250 general and niche magazines. Charges start at $1.50 per article download.

Internet Connections

Members can leave CompuServe at any time, traveling through electronic gateways out of the informational mall that CompuServe has built, onto the Internet at large. To get to the Internet gateway and access Usenet newsgroups, FTP tools, Telnet tools, and the World Wide Web browser, click the GO button and type in INTERNET.

CompuServe's Internet area also provides tools that will allow you to build your own home page on the Web, and supports several professional forums dedicated to Internet business news and issues. The Internet Welcome Center hosts great informational tips and how-to-cruise-the-Net primers for those new to online life.

One caveat about CompuServe: As with any dial-up service, check to see if you can connect without incurring long-distance phone charges from your local phone company. If you live in a rural area where your dial-in occurs through a long-distance node, you may want to limit your use of this service.

PART III

A Writer's Primer to Using the Internet

CHAPTER 14

Finding Your Way Through Cyberspace: *Power-Using Internet Search Engines and Indexes*

Imagine setting out to research the history and lore of typesetting—maybe you need to verify Johannes Gutenberg's birth date. Perhaps you've a different inquiry—you need to look for a list of U.S. chess champions to round out an article on the game of masters. What if your fourth-grader needs to know the state bird of Alabama?

Continue along in your imagining. You are given carte blanche at the New York Public Library—highly regarded as one of the world's greatest repositories of things *bibliotheque*, guarded by its two massive granite lions. Surely, there is no better place to begin and complete a round of research—*whatever* your topic.

But all the rules have changed. Though you have access to the stacks, they're without the familiar Dewey Decimal numberings, and the card catalog is nowhere to be found. Some rogue has torn the covers and bindings from the books, leaving nothing that remotely resembles order. There's an empty chair behind the help desk—budgetary problems, you know. All of this makes your informational search daunting or downright impossible.

Welcome to the Internet, where there's no Dewey Decimal system or its companion card catalog. With literally thousands of new "pages" being added to (and disappearing from) the World Wide Web on a daily basis, how on earth will you find anything—much less anything of value?

What you need is some kind of highly refined search tool with the nose of a thousand bloodhounds. Luckily, such tools exist. Some, of course, are better than others at particular types of things, but all of them can make searching for information on the Internet less frustrating and more productive.

Search Engines, Spiders, and Indexes

Though sometimes lumped together in discussion, a Web index is not a search engine, nor is the reverse true. The various Internet search tools available and freely accessible on the Web are actually built around different concepts. Using the tools most effectively means knowing (at least in part) what they are and how they work.

Keyword Indexes

A keyword index builds a master index of the text content of millions of documents stored on the Web—word by word. Computer software tools known as "spiders" and "robots" roam the wild, wild Web, relentlessly gobbling up words for input into their master indexes. Some of the best known search sites— AltaVista, Infoseek, Lycos—are keyword indexes.

Keyword indexes often boast loudly about the size of their master index, about the number of words and concepts that can be sorted through via their unique online search systems. With keyword indexes, size *does* matter, since a search conducted at a particular site cannot find what does not exist in that site's master index. Keyword indexes are fast and fairly easy to use. When used, they generally return a reliable list of Internet sites that contain one or more of the search terms entered. For example, entering the word "igneous" into a search engine will retrieve a listing of sites that contain that word—everything you've always wanted to know about igneous rocks, and more. Advanced search techniques can make keyword indexes powerful search tools.

AltaVista
http://www.altavista.digital.com

AltaVista, started by Digital's Research Laboratories, is one of the most popular search engines on the Web. With an index of 30 million pages found on 275,600 servers, and 4 million articles from 14,000 Usenet newsgroups, AltaVista's site is accessed more than 23 million times per weekday—can you imagine?

Searching on AltaVista can be confusing at first because the simple default search retrieves documents containing as many of the words and phrases as possible. This default search can result in thousands of documents for you to sift your way through.

AltaVista's site offers a tremendous amount of help for those who want to move beyond the default search and refine their results. Combining the available help with AltaVista's advanced search option will help lower the static and zero in on your more precise search request.

Excite!
http://www.excite.com

Excite! is a full-power search engine that summarizes more than 50 million Web pages and more than two weeks of Usenet newsgroup postings. It boasts more than 61,000 reviews of Web sites written by professional journalists, and an hourly news update service from Reuters. Founded in a garage in September 1993 by six Stanford University graduates who were tired of making "keyword searches," Excite! makes searching for information on the Internet less tiring.

Excite! employs a technique called *concept technology*. Like most search engines, Excite! retrieves documents containing the exact words you entered into the query box; however, it also looks for ideas closely linked to the words in your query. For example, suppose you enter "elderly people financial concerns" in the query box. In addition to finding sites containing those exact words, the search engine will find sites mentioning the economic status of retired people and the financial concerns of senior citizens.

Excite! returns a list of search results with a relevancy ranking. Sites thought to be the most accurate hits according to your query dimensions will have relevancy rankings closer to 100 percent. In addition, many of the listed results will include a "more like this" link following them. Selecting the "more like this" link will reveal more sites similar to the one you liked.

HotBot
http://www.hotbot.com

From the techno-savvy minds of HotWired, the online version of *Wired* magazine, comes HotBot. HotBot was designed to meet the more rigorous research needs of writers and other professionals; this also means that it was designed, at least in part, for users already versed in online search techniques. Although there is some help available here on how to conduct a search, it's on the light side. You might want to master searching techniques by using other indexes and their help features online before tackling HotBot.

HotBot offers options for restricting your online searches by date, location, or media type. A button labeled "Save my settings" enables you to customize the interface so it appears the same way each time you return to HotBot.

InfoSeek
http://www.infoseek.com

Claiming to be "proof of intelligent life on the Net," Infoseek accommodates two types of searches. The basic UltraSeek search is easy to use, accepts natural language questions, and provides a unique feature that allows you to narrow the results of a search. After results have been displayed, you can add additional search modifiers and choose to "search only these results." Besides returning results that contain the search term, the UltraSmart search categorizes the search terms and provides links to related topics and stories. InfoSeek offers lots of help and an uncluttered, easy-to-use interface.

Lycos
http://www.lycos.com

One of the very first search tools on the Internet, Lycos boasts a tremendous database of Web pages by virtue of its longevity. Lycos is the only major search engine to work with Web page abstracts instead of the entire text of a page. Lycos's home page offers a variety of choices. You can search specifically for sound or picture files, people, city information, and more. Additionally, Lycos offers categorical "WebGuides" that allow you to narrow your search to a defined topic: News, Money, Fashion, Entertainment, Government, Business, and a dozen more topics are available.

Subject Directories

A subject directory is a multilevel hierarchy that you can drill your way down through, refining your search with each new level of the subject you choose to explore. Subject directories, like Yahoo!, prescreen Web site content, categorizing sites for you based on their primary broad subject category.

Yahoo!, for example, categorizes sites based on 14 subject hierarchies. If you are at Yahoo! searching for Web sites that archive information on the literary classics, for example, you'd begin your search with the Arts and Humanities category. You'd then work your way down to the particular sub-category of the arts that interested you—literature, then the classics.

Though not as extensive in their listings as keyword sites, if you're looking for information on a specific topic, a subject directory will generally get you there with less distraction. For example, while all of the keyword indexes we searched returned over 1,500 matches for the single keyword search term "igneous," it took us just five mouse clicks in a subject directory to drill down to where we could actually go rock digging on the Web.

Subject directories, by their very nature, are somewhat *subjective*—some more than others. There are directory sites that employ full-time site reviewers who not only categorize, but review and rate various sites much like Siskel and Ebert. Subject directories, even those with no ratings or reviews, require some human involvement and thus are more likely to screen out totally irrelevant content.

All-In-One
http://www.albany.net/allinone

All-In-One is best described as a directory of directories and engines. A compilation of various search tools found on the Internet, All-In-One can be used to search for just about anything on the Web. Because it is an index of other directories and engines, there is no specific search criteria to "better" use All-In-One. As you move through the All-In-One index, you'll find short descriptions of each site and a link to the home page of that site; there, you can read up on specific tips to help narrow your search.

All-In-One is broken down into several groups including the World Wide Web Section, which lists numerous search engines on one page; a General Internet Section covering topics such as newsgroups, advertising, domain names, hotlist databases, learning courses, reference centers, Gopher searches, and so on; and a Specialized Interest Searches section on games, products, sites, and so on.

Look Smart
http://www.looksmart.com

Billing itself as "100,000 flowers, not 60 million weeds," LookSmart is a menu-driven, category/subcategory search. Conceived by a husband-and-wife team who thought there ought to be a better way, LookSmart begins with a listing of ten categories: Computers & Internet, Business & Finance, Reference & Education, Society & Issues, Shopping & Services, Travel & Vacations, Sports & Recreation, Entertainment & Leisure, Health & Fitness, Home, Family & Auto. Each category then cascades out to provide a short list of subcategories. Lists are kept short to facilitate easy selection.

Magellan
http://www.mckinley.com

Magellan is a search directory that also provides site reviews. A search executed at Magellan pulls up Web pages with their accompanying reviews. A star rating system, (e.g., "This is a Magellan 4-Star Site") reveals what a Magellan reviewer thought of the Web site you are about to visit last she or he visited it. The star ratings are provided, in theory, to help you, the searcher, visit the best sites first while simultaneously bypassing the less stellar ones. Unfortunately, all rating systems are subjective, and there is no guarantee that any reviewer's opinion about what makes a site interesting or informative might, in the end, mesh with your own ideas in this same area.

Fifteen directory categories—Arts, Business, Computing, Education, Entertainment, Health, Hobbies, Investing, Life & Style, News & Reference, People Pages, Regional, Science, Shopping, Sports—can be searched through at Magellan.

Yahoo!
http://www.yahoo.com

The best-known subject directory is Yahoo! Started in 1994 by two Stanford University graduate students, Yahoo! soon became synonymous with the phrase "Web search." Organized in a hierarchical manner, Yahoo! begins with 14 main categories—Arts and Humanities; Business and Economy; Computers and Internet; Education; Entertainment; Government; Health; News and Media; Recreation and Sports; Reference; Regional; Science; Social Science; Society and Culture—each of which is then subdivided into appropriate subcategories, then further divided as necessary.

Subject Specialty Indexes

Even more focused and specialized are a growing number of sites that confine their search expertise to a specific subject area. For example, if it's travel information you're looking for, try Map Quest <http://www.mapquest.com>, an interactive atlas and road trip planner; or browse City Search <http://www.citysearch.com> for a guide to sites in major U.S. cities; or click in at Leisure Plan <http:// www.leisureplan.com> to plan your next great escape.

Travel is but the tip of an extensive category iceberg. You'll find specialty indexes devoted to the arts and entertainment, government and politics, business and finance, education, employment, games, sports, computers, cars, science, law, and so on. Many of these indexes are maintained by experts or specialists in their particular fields. For writers, we mention throughout this guide a number of really great specialty indexes to newspapers and other literary items. Specialized indexes combine the keen focus of a subject index with the speed and ease of use of a keyword index—not a bad combination. The following list profiles some of the more interesting specialty indexes on the Web.

Medical World
http://pride-sun.poly.edu

Medical World Search is a unique search site for the field of medicine. Medical World uses a thesaurus of more than 400,000 medical terms to expand or narrow your search, and it performs a full-text search of the major medical sites on the Web. Free registration at the site will remember your last ten queries and last ten result sites visited.

More Like These: C|Net's A to Z List
http://www.search.com

There are far too many specialized search sites to list them all individually here, but an extensive listing of specialized sites is archived off C|Net's Search.Com home page at the A to Z list. C|Net's alphabetical listing is quite thorough. Visit this site to search for all sorts of specialized directories and indexes.

Training and Seminar Locator (TASL)
http://www.tasl.com

This collection of large and well-organized databases helps you locate business-oriented seminars, classes, and conferences, as well as consultants and training materials such as books and videos. Currently listing 484 providers, TASL can be searched for services available on demand, scheduled events, specific products, or specific providers.

Meta Sites

Meta search sites let you do what sounds impossible—search in more than one place at a time. Instead of searching AltaVista OR Excite! OR InfoSeek, you can simultaneously search them ALL. Meta sites send your query to multiple search services. They then combine the results of your search into one large listing for you.

Though meta site searches can result in time saved, there are some serious caveats about searching this way in one fell swoop. First, a meta site's results can be held up by one extremely busy or unavailable service. You may find yourself waiting and waiting at a meta site when Net traffic is most congested. Also, the often extensive help located at each specific search site will not be available to you if you submit your search from a meta site. If you need to be exact in your search, you will lose some of this ability by handing over your search to the querying power of a single-minded machine.

Though specific search tools have differing technologies behind them, many of the Web sites dedicated to helping you search the cyber-ether for your particular minutia combine the best aspects of the various structures. Hybrid sites provide both a subject index and the ability to perform a simple or advanced keyword search within the hierarchy of that subject index. So, you needn't choose fish or fowl—you can have it all!

PUBLISHER MacMillan

TITLE Writer's Guide To Internet Resources

AUTHOR

Phillips

SUBJECT

LOCATION

Writing Ref.

PRICE

C|Net Search.Com
http://www.search.com

A comprehensive and easy-to-use compilation site is C|Net's Search.Com. Search.Com might be considered a "search engine mall," since it provides one-click access to both generalized and specialized search sites. Want to do a general search? Go no further than C|Net's front door, where you can enter a search that will be driven by AltaVista's search engine.

A listing of categories scrolls alphabetically down the left side of Search.Com's home page, making it a snap (or a click) to focus in on categories such as the Arts, Shopping, Government, Finance, or Travel. Selecting a category provides a list of search sites dedicated to your chosen topic, along with icons to represent C|Net's "top picks" in the various areas.

DogPile
http://www.dogpile.com

DogPile differs from other multi-site search tools in its organizational structure. Arfie—DogPile's "work dog"—searches three sites at a time, starting with the "very general index search," which is likely to return a small number of specific, focused results from directory type sites (such as Yahoo!); then moving down the ordered list to the "very specific superengine"—those keyword index sites (like AltaVista) that generally return far too many results to dig through. Arfie searches, returns the results, then on your command, will go back out to fetch some more.

One nice feature that sets DogPile apart from other meta sites is Arfie's ability to know how long to wait for a response at a particular site before turning tail and sniffing elsewhere. If a particular server is down (not an uncommon event on the Net), Arfie will move on after a predetermined time instead of waiting endlessly like a too-faithful pup.

MetaSearch
http://www.metasearch.com

MetaSearch plugs your search term into forms for multiple search sites, but searches must then be submitted one at a time. MetaSearch allows you to specify a search for all or any words entered, a phrase only, or words as part of other words. You can also specify or limit the number of matches or "hits" to be returned. Enter a word or words in MetaSearch, and it copies your terms to search forms for many different search engines, saving you a few keystrokes. MetaSearch queries Yahoo!, AltaVista, InfoSeek, Lycos, WebCrawler, OpenText, and TradeWave, among others.

SavvySearch
http://wagner.cs.colostate.edu:1969

SavvySearch, like DogPile, submits your query to multiple search engines simultaneously. SavvySearch creates a search plan from your query and ranks and groups the various search engines in order of anticipated usefulness. Your search is submitted to the group of best bets. As results are returned, you have the option of submitting to the next group of search engines. SavvySearch's search query form is available in numerous languages including French, Dutch, Italian, Spanish, Korean, Russian, and Esperanto.

Power Searching Tips

World Wide Web search engines and indexes can be employed to find a recipe for peach cobbler or to execute research on the effectiveness of phonetics as a teaching tool in the primary grades. In any case, knowing exactly what you are looking for will tremendously increase your likelihood of finding it on the Net. A good online research strategy begins with your understanding of three crucial things:

1. Know the question(s) you seek to answer.

2. Pre-identify the concept(s) at the heart of those questions.

3. Know the words (including their variations and synonyms) that are central to those concepts.

Good preparation makes for more successful online searching.

Using Boolean Operators—Little Things Mean a Lot

It doesn't matter which tool you choose to search the Net; however, it won't work well if you don't know how to use it properly. Want to do a more effective job of searching the volumes of information on the Net? A little bit of algebra will help. Yes, that's right. Boolean algebra adds power to an Internet keyword search. Don't be put off—Boolean searching actually involves "word" math—the best kind of math for writers.

The basics of Boolean algebra are centered on three small but powerful words—AND, OR, and NOT. Combining one or more of these operators with your search terms will often yield big dividends.

Focusing and Broadening Your Search

Entering the search phrase "George AND Washington" will lead you to information on the first president of the United States, whereas the phrase "George OR Washington" is just as likely to bring you to the state of Washington or John F. Kennedy, Jr.'s editorial effort, *George* magazine. Adding a NOT to the phrase, as in "George AND Washington NOT Carver" would help exclude that famed scientist who made magic with the peanut.

In addition to the "big little three"—AND, OR, NOT—many search engines also employ terms known as proximity indicators. Words such as NEAR, ADJACENT TO, and FOLLOWED BY add some power and direction to your search. Thus a query phrased, "George FOLLOWED BY Washington" would exclude those documents mentioning George Bush in the first paragraph and Washington Irving in the last.

Not all sites make use of the plus and minus signs, but they are used by some of the major search systems, such as AltaVista. These signs tell the search engine which terms must (+) and must not (–) be present in the returned documents. When using these options, do not leave any space between the sign and the word.

Searching for George AND Washington +Carver is more likely to yield information on George Washington Carver, the peanut wizard. A search for George AND Washington –Carver will keep the peanuts out of the mix.

Punctuate Correctly!

As far as most search engines are concerned, ordering a search on the three consecutive words, internal combustion engine, is not the same as entering these same words in quotation marks as a group, "internal combustion engine." Putting quotation marks around a set of words tells an automated engine to search only for this string of words as they appear together.

A query in quotations marks to find sites on the "internal combustion engine" will return sites that have information only on the internal combustion engine. But leave out those quotation marks, and what you may get are sites that have the word or main concept "internal," as well as sites on "combustion," and sites on "engines." Instead of coming up with exactly what you wanted—sites on the internal combustion engine—you will have leads to things as scattered as spontaneous combustion, internal revenue service, and antique locomotive engines.

Parentheses ( ) can be used to group portions of Boolean queries together for more complicated queries. For example, to find documents that contain the word "fruit" and either the word "peach" or the word "pear," enter this query command: fruit AND (peach OR pear).

Know How Your Chosen Search Site Works

Each search site, no matter the type, has a default mode of operation for a basic search. Some sites operate with a default OR search, while other sites are in the default AND mode. Entering a pair of search terms without a Boolean operator will yield different results depending on the site's default mode.

Using the Advanced Options and Help

Many search sites offer an advanced search option that will allow you to override the default settings. Using the advanced options will help you customize your search.

Don't shy away from the Help buttons found on most search site home pages. There is often extensive help available, just a click away. A few minutes spent getting to know more about your preferred search tool is time that will be well spent as you dig for your chosen needles in the vast informational haystack.

Some of the larger sites allow you to create your own customized version of their start page—starting, perhaps, on the advanced search page rather than the default. Such customization can be altered as needed and can help save time when actively searching for information.

CHAPTER 15

Browsing the
World Wide Web

The World Wide Web, also referred to as the WWW or *the Web*, is the part of the Internet that is available to your computer via HTTP or Hypertext Transfer Protocol. So what is hypertext, and why transfer it? And why has the area of the Internet known as the World Wide Web become so popular? All good questions!

The Web presents information as a series of documents, called *Web pages.* These pages have been specially prepared using Hypertext Markup Language (HTML). Using HTML, the document's author codes sections of the document to "point" to other information resources. These specially coded sections of text or pictures are referred to as *hypertext links.* Users viewing a Web page can select or "click on" coded hypertext to retrieve or connect to the information that the link points to. The text is "hyper" because it doesn't just sit there—it does something! Hypertext is at the heart of any point-and-click multimedia system.

When you click on a link in a hypertext Web document or picture, you effectively say to your computer "take me there" or "get me that." HTTP and HTML take care of the details. Unlike the earlier Net tools, like FTP (File Transfer Protocol), you don't have to type in strings of computer command lingo to get things done—to retrieve files or to jump from place to place on the Net. These computer commands are "coded into" or buried behind the point-and-click pictorial interface that has made the World Wide Web the sexiest, simplest to navigate, and fastest growing area of the Net.

Because it can incorporate graphics and "understands" other Internet protocols such as FTP, Gopher, and Telnet, the Web provides an easy-to-use, graphical interface for accessing resources available via these other protocols also.

Understanding the Ubiquitous URL

The "links" or "addresses" that are used to navigate the Web are called *Uniform Resource Locators* or *URLs* (pronounced "earl"). An URL is the standard address of an object on the Internet. Like a street address, an URL has several parts. To get to a particular site on the Web or any area of the Net, you need to know its URL or Internet address. You input the URL address into the software that you will use to navigate the Web. This software is called a *Web browser*. To understand URLs and how to navigate the Web, let's look first at how to read an URL.

Sample URL:
http://www.together.net/~lifelong/index.html

The part before the first colon (in this case, "http") specifies the access scheme or protocol. This tells your Web browser what type of access or resource is being looked for. HTTP is the most common protocol used on the World Wide Web and the Net, but it is not the only one. Other older non-Web protocols include FTP, Gopher, and Telnet.

The first two slashes in an URL introduce the host name. This is the name that has been given to the specific computer that holds the information you're after. The host name includes the name of the machine ("www"), the domain name ("together") and the top-level domain ("net"). In the preceding URL, the host name is "www.together.net."

The top-level domain describes the type of organization that maintains the page(s) you are about to access. The major categories for top-level domains on the Net are:

COM—commercial entities

EDU—four year colleges and universities

NET—organizations directly involved in Internet operations, such as network providers and network information centers

ORG—miscellaneous organizations that don't fit any other category, such as nonprofit groups

GOV—United States Federal Government entities

MIL—United States military

COUNTRY CODES—two letter abbreviations for particular countries. For example, "UK" for United Kingdom or "FR" for France.

The next part of the URL is the pathname to a specific file. In the previous example, the path points to the index file, often called the home page, for Lifelong Learning's Web site. Keep in mind that the path- and filename may be case sensitive. INDEX.HTML is not the same as index.html. Pay close attention to the use of lowercase and uppercase letters in any URL address!

The "generic" anatomy of an URL is:

protocol://server-name.domain-name.top-level domain/ directory/filename

Knowing a little something about the structure of URLs can help you avoid some Internet frustration. The Internet still is—and likely always will be—in a state of flux. Resources that you find in one place might pack up and steal away in the middle of the night to another place—another server or another file name.

For example, suppose you were using the Internet to shop around for some home exercise equipment—a stairmaster—and found some information at <http://www.healthy.com/exercise/stair.html>, but when you try to return to that URL or specific address, you get an error message that says "File Not Found." Hmm . . . seems the fine folks at healthy.com did some file shifting overnight; though the information is still there on the host server, your URL no longer points to the right place. In fact, they have moved your file to "stairmaster.html," renaming the file in the process to better fit their growing file categorization scheme.

What should you do when you get a "File Not Found" message at a site where you know a specific file used to live? First, don't despair! Try pruning the URL back to just the protocol and host name (http://www.healthy.com). In our sample case, this would bring you to healthy.com's default home page. Once there, you could follow the master table of contents or index usually given on the main page to find the new filename given to your stairmaster informational file.

Remember, the Internet is far from a perfect system. Tens of thousands of various computers and servers are "stitched" or networked together to form the Internet. At any time, individual servers can go down, or major disruptions can occur in line transmissions. Or people can switch servers, moving themselves and their sites across country in the process. As you learn to cruise the Net, and the World Wide Web, be prepared to get error messages. Understand that sometimes an error message simply means that a file has been moved. At other times, it may mean that a server has gone down—often temporarily—so you may get a "try again later" message.

If you can't access an URL the first time you try, don't panic. Try again later, or the next day. It may simply be an error caused by too much Internet traffic at peak access hours. If you cannot access an URL after several tries, visit one of the Net search engine sites, like AltaVista <http://www.altavista.digital.com>, and conduct a search on the site you are trying to access. If the site has indeed moved, a search engine like AltaVista will quickly pull up the new URL.

Building a Better Browser

The tool, client, or software you will use to access the World Wide Web is called a Web browser. A browser is a piece of software that acts as an interface between the user and the inner-workings of the Internet, specifically the World Wide Web. Browsers are also referred to as Web clients.

A browser can be graphical or text based, but these days they are generally driven by graphics or pictures. The very first Web browser, Lynx, is a text-only tool that allows you to move from hyperlink to hyperlink using keyboard commands. Though it did the job quite well in the early days of the Web when most of the content was just text, Lynx has been relegated to the basement of

Internet tools. Jazzy multimedia-capable graphical Web browsers are the rule. Graphical browsers make the World Wide Web a point-and-click wonderland of picture and sound these days.

The heart of a Web browser is simple. You give the browser an URL by typing it into a dialog box. The browser then connects to the host machine. It requests, receives, and then obediently displays the retrieved information on your home computer.

The Web incorporates hypertext, photographs, sound, video, and so on that can be fully experienced through a graphical browser. Browsers often include "helper applications," which are special software programs that are needed to display images, hear sounds, or run animation sequences. These helper applications may be automatically invoked by your browser when you select a link to a resource that requires them.

Just as all cars provide transportation, all Web browsers do the same thing: They transfer hypertext across the Internet. Attempts to capitalize on the explosion of Web popularity brought a number of graphical Web browsers to market early on. All but two have faded into the distance: The two big names in Web browsers these days are Netscape Navigator and Microsoft Internet Explorer.

Netscape Navigator (or Netscape for short) <http://www.netscape.com> was developed in early 1993 by Marc Andreessen and a team of students and staff at the National Center for Supercomputing Applications (NCSA). Microsoft Internet Explorer (Internet Explorer or MSIE for short) <http://www. microsoft.com/ie> was developed by the Microsoft Corporation and can be used on PCs running Windows 3.1 or better, or on Macintosh systems. Both browsers undergo constant development and growth as the two giants fight the "browser wars."

As the two battle for market share, they are more alike than different. Each offers the same basic functionality and is used in the same way. The basic browser screen has a menu bar, a toolbar or button bar, a location field at the top portion of the screen, and a status or progress indicator along the bottom. The majority of screen real estate is the content viewing area. Whether you use Netscape's product, Microsoft's, or another graphical browser, navigation these days is point-and-click.

Saving Bookmarks and Favorites

Imagine this: You've spent 30 minutes searching the Web for information about a particular topic. You have finally found an extremely useful Web site, but now you don't have the time to explore it. How will you ever find this page again when you have more time? You could write down the URL for the Web page, being careful to note spelling and capitalization, and hope that you'll find that little scrap of paper next week—or you could bookmark it (Netscape) or add it to your favorites list (MSIE).

When a bookmark or favorite is added, your browser software "writes down" the URL for you in a file saved on your home computer's hard drive. You can then easily access this URL at any time later. Returning to a bookmarked or favorite site is as simple as opening the menu item on your browser and clicking on the link. Using the bookmark or favorite function on your browser can save you a lot of time and headaches. It is one of the first features of your browser you'll want to master if you intend to research online a great deal.

Browsing in Your Sleep

With so much out there, it's hard to keep up with the constant stream of information, and it's easy to feel the overload. There's so much information—much of it changing every few weeks—that special tools have been recently developed that allow your Web browser to go out on the Net and gather information for you while you sleep. Known as *off-line readers* or *Internet agents*, these new tools can help you stay a step ahead of the endless stream of constantly changing Web site information.

Though they vary to some extent, all of the off-line readers follow the same basic principle. You spend a bit of time telling the reader what and how much you want it to go out and retrieve for you, then you schedule the little monster to go fetch Web pages while you sleep. The agent obediently downloads the chosen Web sites to your computer's hard drive. You are then free to browse the captured information at your leisure.

Obviously one great advantage to this is that it can be a no-grunt way for you to keep up to date on information as it changes at Web sites that you'd otherwise have to log onto and visit every week or so. Another advantage is that traveling on the Information Superhighway can be an uncertain adventure. Internet traffic can be slow at times—impossible at others. Instead of spending your time trying to connect to a Web site, you can let your computer grunt away at it while you sleep.

Some of the current offerings in the off-line reader market are FreeLoader (which truly is free) <http://www.freeloader.net>; WebWhacker <http://www. ffg.com>; SurfBot <http://www.surflogic.com>; WebEx <http://www. travsoft.com/products/webex>; FlashSite <http://www.incontext.com>; and NetAttache <http://www.tympani.com>. Visit these sites to explore more about off-line readers and to "test-drive" sample or freeware versions.

CHAPTER 16

Finding and Retrieving Material on the Information Dirt Road: *Telnet, FTP, Archie, Gopher, and Veronica*

Despite the media-proclaimed "birth" of the Information Superhighway in 1993, the Internet has been widely used as a research and information transfer tool since the early 1970s. Some might say that the Net pre-1993 was an ugly duckling, given that access was usually gained from a dumb monochrome monitor by typing in a series of arcane computer commands. Before the birth of the great graphical point-and-click World Wide Web system (circa 1993), you had to know some computer command lingo to travel along the Information Superhighway.

Once you were on the Net back in the Dark Ages, there were no TV-like multimedia screens with dancing icons to entertain you. There were simple hierarchical trees of informational files that you could search through at places like libraries and research institutes. It was more of an Information Dirt Road than a Superhighway. Still, search-and-retrieval tools developed in the Dark Ages of the Net continue to have great use today if power researching is truly your intent. In the following pages, you'll find a primer on tools other than your Web browser that can get you around the great vast cyberspace.

All of the early Internet search tools were issued in black and white. They were plain but extremely effective, like the beginning of *The Wizard of Oz*. When you logged onto your Internet account, you got a black screen with white or amber text. Then you had to type in commands to run various programs. Some Internet users still log into these "shell" accounts; the search tools that worked in these Dark Ages, pre–World Wide Web and jazzy graphics, still work today.

The explosion in the use of graphical Web browsers has not done away with these early tools or informational back roads. All of the tools and protocols described here can also be accessed using most Web browsers. For example, you can type a Gopher address into a Web browser, and in most cases get to a Gopher site that way. Why bother, then, with learning more about pre-Web search tools and archive spaces? Sometimes a specialized tool for a particular task is stronger, quicker, and easier to use. Also, knowing how to use tools like FTP and Telnet will increase your research muscle once you are online.

By its nature, the Internet is no more than a multitude of computers that are connected together. Most of the time, the information you're after exists on another computer. The trick is getting to it. Here are several ways to find the information you are looking for in addition to using your Web browser.

Telnet

Telnet is one of the original building blocks of the Internet. Though it lacks the graphical flash and dazzle that brought overnight fame to the Web, it remains an essential tool for researchers. Telnet is simply a remote log-on procedure. It allows you to log onto another computer and use it as if you were sitting right at the terminal of that remote machine. Telnet gives you "hands-on" access to online databases, archives, public-access catalogs, libraries, and more—worldwide. Early on, Telnet was the only way to create an interactive session with another computer.

Unlike the highly touted World Wide Web, a Telnet session is all text, no graphics. While this may sound boring, you may be impressed with the increased speed of information access if you bypass your Web browser, using Telnet instead to log into the information you're after.

To Telnet to another computer, you need a Telnet tool. Many personal computer systems include a graphical Telnet tool. Your Internet service provider (ISP) account may provide you with one, and there are a number of Telnet tools available as free shareware. Along with a Telnet tool, you will need the Telnet address of the computer you want to connect to. An excellent listing of public Telnet addresses including libraries, shareware archives, and research document banks, is available at the Electronic Frontier Foundation's Extended Guide to the Internet <http://ftn.net/eff/eeg-96.html#SEC97>.

To Telnet to the Dante Project at Dartmouth College, a full-text search and retrieval database of Dante's Divine Comedy, *La Commedia*, and more than 600 years of commentary, you would Telnet to the address <lib.dartmouth.edu>. Once connected to the Dartmouth College Library Online System, you'd type "connect dante" to access the Dante Project, a joint effort of Dartmouth, Princeton University, and the Dante Society of America. Once there, you can perform sophisticated searches in English, Latin, or Italian. On-screen prompts will help you move through the information and end the session once you've found what you were after.

Dartmouth's library is one among thousands. Inter-Link provides Telnet addresses to academic, research, law, medical, and public library catalogs around the world. Many of these public library catalogs have since adopted a graphical gateway or entry. You can access them also these days via the World Wide Web if you have the address and a Web browser.

FTP

Sometimes, working with information on another computer is what you need to do, like searching the online catalog of a public library via Telnet. Other times, there are files on another computer that you will want to have copied directly onto your own computer. That's when FTP, File Transfer Protocol, becomes the tool of choice. Like all things Internet, FTP involves a connection to another computer. Once connected, you find the file or files you're looking for, then download a copy to your own computer.

There are millions of files available for transfer. Many are free or demonstration versions of various computer programs. Others are archives of text data, computer graphics, sounds, movies, shareware programs—you name it, it's out there!

Like Telnet, FTP has been around for a while, and it is available on shell or institutional accounts by typing "ftp" at the prompt. Most home users, however, will work with one of the various graphical applications of file-transfer programs. A dedicated FTP tool connects you to a public FTP server and lets you browse your way through the files available. Most Web browsers also have the ability to connect to FTP servers.

Most public FTP sites support "anonymous FTP," allowing anyone to log on with the username "anonymous" and any password (netiquette says use your e-mail address as a password for anonymous FTP sessions). As an anonymous guest at the site, your access will be limited to those areas deemed public, but that's where the goodies you're after are generally stored. After connecting to an anonymous FTP site, you can move into subdirectories to view listings of the files stored there. Master index files will catalog the various files available, sometimes providing brief descriptions of the contents of these files also.

One very rich FTP site for writers is the Reading Room at the University of Maryland. FTP to the address <ftp://info.umd.edu>, then move down the subdirectory structure to /inforM/EdRes/ReadingRoom. There, you'll find The On-Line Books Page, a searchable database of more than 1,800 online books. You'll also encounter Project Gutenberg, the Boston Book Review, Electronic and Online Journals, and electronic versions of classic works from Rudyard Kipling to Virginia Woolf. There's even a Fairy Tales directory. A searchable listing of public FTP sites can be found on the World Wide Web at <http://the.list>.

Archie

Derived from the word "archive," not the freckle-faced comic strip character, Archie helps you find individual files on the Internet—no small task with the burgeoning number of files available for downloading all over the world. Developed by the School of Computer Science at McGill University in Montreal,

Canada, Archie keeps track of more than 2 million files at more than a thousand File Transfer Protocol (FTP) sites. Think of Archie as a master directory or search engine to public FTP sites.

Suppose you're shopping around for a computerized calendar program, and a friend tells you about a shareware program called Time and Chaos available for free through FTP. The name seems fitting; now how do you find it? In order to use Archie, you have to know the filename of the program you're after. For instance, the filename for Time and Chaos is something like "tchaoxxx.zip," where "xxx" is the software version number. To locate where you can find and download a free copy of Time and Chaos on the Net via FTP, you'd turn to Archie and execute a search for the filename—in this case, "tchao."

If you aren't using an open shell account where you can access Archie by simply typing it at the prompt, you can Telnet to an Archie server. In the Midwest, for example, you could type <telnet archie.unl.edu> to connect to the Telnet server at the University of Nebraska. Log on as Archie, and you're ready to search for files.

Another Archie alternative is ArchiePlex on the World Wide Web. Provided by NASA Lewis Research Center, ArchiePlex is at <http://www.lerc.nasa.gov/archieplex/doc/form.html>. Enter your search term, and ArchiePlex will scour anonymous FTP sites worldwide in search of your chosen files.

Gopher

Born at the University of Minnesota and named for their team mascot, Gopher, the Internet tool, provides an interconnected series of text menus that allow you to "burrow" down through various levels of information to find what you're after.

Prior to the advent of the World Wide Web, Gopher was the be-all and end-all of Internet connectivity. Organized and easy to navigate, Gopher simplified the Internet information search for early netizens. Graphical Gopher tools, such as HGopher, made your tunneling adventure as easy as clicking your mouse to move from one site to another.

These days, Web browsers, like Netscape, can also connect to Gopher sites. You simply type the Gopher address of the site you want to visit into the address box on your Web browser. When you connect to a Gopher site, you will be presented with a set of menus offering various choices. Choose the menu item that covers the category of your search and you'll then be taken down to the next menu level. Choose one of these new menu levels and you're likely to find yourself at another menu level. Sooner or later, the choices are specific text or binary files. You then choose the file you came to retrieve.

The best starting place for Gopher exploration is Gopher Jewels at <gopher: //cwis.usc.edu/11/Other_Gophers_and_Information_Resources/Gopher-Jewels>. Gopher Jewels offers lots of how-to help and an extensive listing of public Gophers organized by subject. Subject categories include education, economics, engineering, government, health, law, libraries, science, and research.

Another good starting place for Gopher digging adventures is the site maintained by Washington and Lee University in Lexington, Virginia, at <gopher://liberty.uc.wlu.edu>. WLU's Gopher is well organized and easy to navigate. It allows you to search for Gophers by subject, or to browse through a listing of public Gophers worldwide.

Veronica

Veronica stands for Very Easy Rodent-Oriented Net-Wide Index to Computerized Archives. *Rodent-oriented* refers to the way in which Veronica works with the Internet's Gopher system. What Archie does for FTP, Veronica does for Gopher. Veronica serves as an extremely helpful master search directory to public Gopher archives worldwide.

Although a Gopher is easy to use, it can be cumbersome. You may follow one menu choice and burrow down through layer after layer, but if the material you want is down another Gopher hole or server, you will have to dig your way back up and out before heading down a different hole. It pays, then, to know as much as possible about what you are after, and where to burrow, before you head down a specific Gopher hole.

Veronica to the rescue. Veronica searches "Gopherspace" for items that match any search term you might specify. Veronica finds all the Gopher menu items that contain your search term and presents you with a master list. Suppose you're looking for a chocolate cake recipe. Just type whatever subject or term you want, in this case "chocolate," then hit the Enter key. Veronica will investigate all available Gopher sites, displaying all entries that mention "chocolate" in their menu titles. If you enter more than one search term, like "chocolate cake," Veronica assumes you are using an "AND" qualifier and points you to Gopher menu items containing both words.

Though a very useful tool for organizing comprehensive Gopher searches, Veronica has two drawbacks. Veronica can "see" only the Gopher menu titles—not the contents of the file. There is no guarantee that a file will bear a name that is true to its contents. (Remember, Gopher files can be maintained on hundreds of different servers worldwide. Not everyone titles or categorizes computer files in the same way!) Also, she's a busy woman—during peak hours, you're likely to have trouble logging onto a Veronica site.

Bibliography

Arnzen, Michael. "Cyber Citations: Documenting Internet Sources Presents Some Thorny Problems." *Internet World*, September 1996, pp. 72–74.

Auletta, Ken. "Annals of Communication: The Reeducation of Michael Kinsley." *The New Yorker*, May 13, 1996, pp. 58–73.

Burks, John. "Web Guide Magazines Vie for Readership." *New York Times CyberTimes*, November 25, 1996. http://search.nytimes.com/search/daily/bin/fastweb?getdoc+site+site+7753+1+wAAA+John%7EBurks (May 16, 1997).

Carl, Jeremy. "There's a Crack in the Utne Lens." *Web Week*, November 1995, p. 56.

Furr, Joel. "The Ups and Downs of Newsgroups." *Internet World*, November 1995, pp. 58–60.

Gleick, Elizabeth. "Read All About It." *Time*, October 21, 1996, pp. 66–69.

Hamilton, Denise. "Hart of the Gutenberg Galaxy." *Wired*, February 1997, pp. 108–118.

Hart, Anne. *Cyberscribes 1: The New Journalists*. San Diego, California: Ellipsys International Publications, 1997.

Hayes, Colin. *Paperless Publishing*. New York: McGraw Hill, 1994.

Holzberg, Carol. "At Your Service: Custom News Services Track the Topics You Specify." *Internet World*, May 1996, pp. 46–52.

Krantz, Michael. "Amazonian Challenge." *Time*, April 14, 1997, p. 71.

Macavinta, Courtney. "The Net as Venue—for Books." January 17, 1997. http://www.news.com/News/Item/0,4,7145,4000.html (April 16, 1997).

O'Leary, Mick. *The Online 100: Online Magazine's Field Guide to the 100 Most Important Online Databases.* Wilton, Connecticut: Pemberton Press, 1995.

Phillips, Vicky. "Earn Your Master's Virtually." *Internet World*, September 1996, pp. 67–70.

Phillips, Vicky. "Modem Cum Laude: College Life Is a Screen." *Connect-Time*, March 1997, pp. 6–7.

Phillips, Vicky. "These Are Not Your Mother's Magazines." *New Media Week*, August 1997, p. 2.

Phillips, Vicky and Cindy Yager. *The Best Distance Learning Graduate Schools: Earn Your Degree without Leaving Home.* New York: Princeton Review, 1997.

Quittner, Joshua. "Man Bites Web: Information Online is a Different Beast That Won't Devour the News." *Time,* October 21, 1996, p. 70.

Rawlins, Gregory. "Technology's Impact on the Publishing Industry Over the Next Decade." November 1991. http://www.obs-us.com/obs/english/papers/rawlins.htm (March 10, 1997).

Reddick, Randy and Elliot King. *The Online Journalist.* New York: Harcourt Brace, 1996.

Reid, Calvin. "Salon: Big-Name Writers on the Web." *Publishers Weekly*, November 27, 1995, p. 14.

Rheingold, Howard. *The Virtual Community.* Reading, Massachusetts: Addison-Wesley, 1993.

Savetz, Kevin. "The Medium Is the Matrix." *Internet World*, April 1995, pp. 70–74.

Schiesel, Seth. "Some Media Organizations Pull the Plug on Web Sites." *New York Times CyberTimes.* March 25, 1997. http://search.nytimes.com/search/daily/bin/fastweb?getdoc+site+site+4370+0+wAA. (May 15, 1997).

Slatalla, Michelle. "An Online Publishing Reality Check." *Netguide*, August 1996, pp. 83–90.

Index

D

H

G

I

T

V

U

W

X

Y

Z